Contemporary Piano Method
book 1A

by Margaret Brandman

Exclusive distributors for Australia and New Zealand
Encore Music Distributors
227 Napier St, Fitzroy VIC 3065 Australia
Phone +61 3 9415 6677
Facsimile +61 3 9415 6655
Email sales@encoremusic.com.au

This book © Copyright 2017 by Margaret Brandman trading as Jazzem Music
46 Gerrale St, Cronulla NSW 2230 Australia
ISBN 978-0-949683-52-6
ORDER NUMBER MMP 8075
International copyright secured (APRA/AMCOS). All rights reserved.

Unauthorised reproduction of any part of this publication by any means,
including photocopying, is an infringement of copyright.

CONTEMPORARY PIANO METHOD

INTRODUCTION

This method is designed to equip the student with the necessary skills to play both Classical and Modern (Popular and Jazz) music, with ease and understanding while giving experience in skills required for both classical and contemporary examination syllabi. The piano method is the central core of an integrated course which provides materials for ear-training (CD's and workbooks), theory, improvisation and repertoire pieces in all styles.

The methodology incorporates various learning styles or modalities, including:
- aural training
- spatial reasoning - visual, aural and tactile
- colour - to impart the meanings of the duration of the notes
- visualisation and the use of pictorial representations of intervals
- the gestalt approach (whole view)
- knowledge of keyboard geography
- shape and pattern reading
- harmonic analysis
- improvisation
- gross motor actions to understand direction concepts and for musical technique

A valuable feature of the method is the accompanying *Contemporary Piano Method* DVD in which many of the special teaching techniques are demonstrated. The DVD is useful for students and teachers alike.

The simplified interval approach
The series introduces a versatile and flexible way to read music through a simplified *interval* approach which combines the aural, tactile, vocal and visual aspects of music into one neat package. Even more effective than the usual numerical system for interval sizes, use of the easy interval language shown in this book can help the swift transference of the picture of the distance between two notes (interval) to the *feeling in the hand* and the *aural impression of the sound*. This means that students no longer have to look down at the keyboard to search for each note and consequently rely more on other faculties such as ear and touch, leaving the eyes free to follow the music. In addition, the simplified interval language avoids confusion between numbers for fingering and numbers for counting.

A multi-level teaching system
This book can be used for complete beginners from the age of twelve and up, or for those youngsters who have completed the *Junior Primer* (begin on p 14).
It is also useful for experienced players, wishing to improve their existing reading skills by learning to *transpose* and play easily in all major keys (begin on p 16).

Anchor Points
In this book the notes C and F are used as signpost notes. As the Cs are easy to locate on the keyboard layout, both visually and by touch, this also allows the interval reading system to be extended to reading above and below the staff and into C Clef.

Follow the flow
The system encourages students to see music as a flowing chart while moving around the keys by means of spatial reasoning, tactile response and a consistent use of aural skills for pre-hearing and correction. As soon as two notes are played in succession the ear begins to recognise the motif or essential idea of a song and can build on that perception. In the accompanying materials (*Dexter's Easy Piano Pieces* and *Daily Dexter-Flexers*) the sizes of the intervals are represented pictorially by characters on staircases to impart the idea of how many keys are stepped along or skipped over.

Seeing the whole view (gestalt) - shape and pattern reading
Reading by following the flow of the intervals and the contour of the musical line, enhances shape and pattern reading (for example chords and scalic passages) as an aid to sight reading and speed learning of pieces. It also provides the foundation for the understanding of keys, chords and the harmonic structure of a piece.

Understanding Harmonic Structure
A unique feature of this course is that students are actively engaged in the task of discovering the underlying harmonic structure of music, using the information to speed up the learning process, build an aural awareness of keys and chords, and to use as a basis for improvisation. In Books 1A and 1B students are required to discover the key of each piece, work out the Primary Chords in the key and then locate them in the music. This is a most important factor in the student's ability to learn music for themselves and gain professional skills.

Even more flexibility and versatility
Once students understand the easy concepts and can transfer the message to their fingers, they are able to:
    a) play with *both hands together* more readily as the reading for both parts uses similar information, rather than two sets of note names.
    b) play on the *staff lines* or on *leger lines* with equal ease.
    c) *transpose* to various areas of the keyboard. If white note patterns are shifted they can produce interesting 'modal' sounds.
    d) *transpose to all keys* - provided that the scale patterns on the keyboard are learnt as a pre-requisite.
    e) *sing the intervals* as they play using the language of Step, Skip etc. This will enable them to *learn to sight sing* and at the same time quickly *develop aural perception*.

Easy ways to conceptualise rhythm and rhythm notation
The use of diagrams to be coloured in and then clapped helps students to quickly associate a concrete meaning to the new language of music rhythm notation and establish a body feel for timing. The use of colour, spatial concepts and the tactile information transferred by the act of colouring, brings into play many accelerated learning concepts.

Direction concepts
Using the *gestalt view* of intervals, students are more readily able to see a larger section of music in one glance so that the *combined direction* of the notes for both hands becomes more obvious. This helps greatly in the early stages of learning in the actual process of co-ordinating the hands and relaying the message to the fingers.

Keyboard patterns for scales and keys
To simplify playing in all twelve keys and transposition, Books 1A and 1B encourage a thorough knowledge of all Major Scales and Chords and their usage in all types of music through using the keyboard pattern approach to scales along with the gestalt approach to finding them on the instrument. Students are required to close eyes and visualise their hands on the keyboard pattern for the key before reading the music. Refer to the graphic on page 67.

Even more information on the scale patterns can be found in the accompanying scale book:
'Playing Made Easy'- Pictorial Patterns for Keyboard Scales and Chords.

Guide Notes for Teachers
A page of background information and suggestions for the expansion of the topics is given on page 65 of this book.

For more detailed information on the ideas and information in this series, refer to the website:

www.margaretbrandman.com

Margaret Brandman (Dr)
PhD.Mus/Arts., F.Mus.Ed ASMC., F.Comp. ASMC.,
B.Mus.,(Syd) T.Mus.A., L.Perf. ASMC.,
A.Mus.A., Hon.FNMSM. (UK)
International Woman of the Year for Music (2003)

INTEGRATED SUPPORT MATERIALS FOR THIS LEVEL

PRACTICAL

- Contemporary Piano Method DVD
- The Geometry of the Piano and the Symmetry of the Hands DVD

Technical Work
- Pictorial Patterns for Keyboard Scales and Chords
- Daily Dexter-Flexers

Repertoire
Enjoy playing the pieces in these books as you consolidate the skills learned in CPM 1A:
- Junior Trax
- Dexter's Easy Piano Pieces
- Hot Trax
- Christmas Favourites
- Twelve Timely Pieces

THEORY

- Contemporary Theory Primer
- Contemporary Theory Workbooks – 1 & 2
- Contemporary Chord Workbook – Book 1

EAR-TRAINING

- *Contemporary Aural Course*
- Preparatory Level
- Set One
- Set Two

CONTENTS

Meeting a Piano for the first time 6
Seating and Hand Position 7
The Keyboard and Fingers. 8
Reading Intervals 9
Feeling Intervals 10
Writing Intervals 11
Finding Middle C 12
Note values 13
Playing in Hand Position 1 14
Playing in Hand Position 2 15
Intervals for the Advanced Player 16
Hand Positions 3 & 4 .... 17 & 18
Double Hand Positions (2 Hands together) /
Other books to use 19
Counting and Colouring 20
No. 1 *Movin' Around* 21
No. 2 *Feelin' The Keys* 22
No. 3 *Finger Play.* /
No. 4 *Doin' The Step-Skip Rag* 23
Hand Positions 5 & 6 24
No. 5 *Movin' Down The Line* 25
C Major Scale 26
Sharp, Flat, Natural 27
Tones and Semitones /
G Major Scale 28
C Contrary Motion Scale /
No. 6 *Swinging Along* 29
Hand Positions 7 & 8 30
No. 7 *Tired Feet* /
No. 8 *Singing High* 31
Degree Numbers and Degree Names 32
The Major Chord 33
No. 9 *Derry Ding Ding Dason* 34
Crossover Positions /
No. 10 *Keep On Skippin'* (C Major) 35
Ties / No. 11 *Tie One On* (G Major) 36

No. 12 *Promenading* (G Major) 37
D, A and E Major Scales 38
Key Signatures / Sixths 39
Primary Chords 40
How to Spot Chords 41
No. 13 *Three For The Road* (D Major) 42
Anacrusis /
No. 14 *Struttin' On 6th Street* (D Major) 43
Sevenths and Octaves 44
Listen here! /
Changing Hand Positions 45
Octave Hopping /
Interval Reading using Accidentals 46
No. 15 *River Song* (A Major) 47
How To Play Staccato 48
No. 16 *Crisp And Crunchy* (A Major) 49
B and F Major Scales /
Broken Chords .... 50 & 51
12-Bar Blues 52
No. 17 *'A' Waltz* (A Major) 53
B Flat & E Flat Major Scales & Chords. . 54 & 55
No. 18 *Space Invaders* (A Major) /
Time-Bars 56
No. 19 *Kum Ba Ya* 57
A Flat & D Flat Major Scales & Chords 58
Instant Transposition /
No. 20 *Love Somebody* 59
Quavers /
No. 21 *Seventh Heaven* (E Major) 60
No. 22 *Octavius' Opus* (E Major) 61
F Sharp Major Scale 62
Cycle of Fifths 63
Chromatic Scale 64
Guide Notes for Teachers................. 65
Practice Routine/Scale Fingering Summary..... 66
Keyboard Scale Patterns and Chord Shapes 67

Meeting a Piano for the first time.

Beginners would be wise to follow all these steps and those who already play may like to check these points if they are having trouble with their technique.

If you are playing an upright or a grand piano, or even the Fender Rhodes, it is a good idea to have a look inside the instrument at the strings (on the Rhodes, the tines) and the hammers and dampers to see what happens when you depress a key. You will discover that as the key is depressed, the hammer hits the strings and the dampers lift off. As you then release the key, the hammer has already bounced off and the dampers replace themselves on the strings, cutting off the sound.

With electronic instruments such as the Hammond Organ and synthesizers, the touch is much lighter as the key does not have the hammer mechanism the acoustic piano has. Electric pianos such as the Fender Rhodes try to retain the original piano hammer mechanism and others such as the Wurlitzer and Yamaha try to simulate the touch of the acoustic piano with a built in resistance in the keys.

Once you are familiar with how the sound is produced you can begin to approach the instrument.

(1) A model of the mechanism of a Grand Piano key.

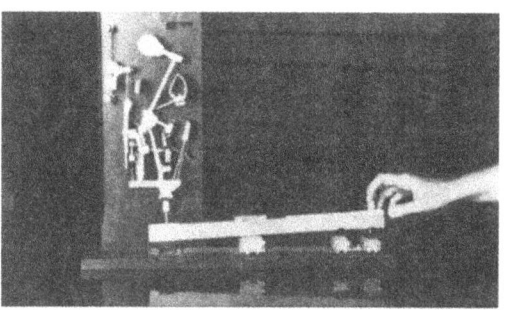

(2) A model of the mechanism of an Upright Piano key.

The key at rest.

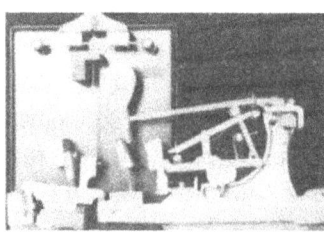

Half way.

As the hammer hits the strings.

View a demonstration on the *Contemporary Piano Method DVD* – Piano Mechanics (6.54)

Figure 1

ASPECTS OF PLAYING

SEATING

Make sure your seating is correct; piano stools should be backless and flat topped, i.e. not sloping. Sit toward the front of the stool so that your weight is forward and place your legs comfortably apart with your feet flat on the floor. (For a small child, place some old phone books on the floor so his feet can rest flat on them.) If you need to, push the chair a little further backwards. From this position you can easily reach the pedals and the extremities of the piano without losing your balance. Make sure also that you are sitting at the right height (a cushion or a couple of books might help) so that your hand position will be a comfortable and natural one.

> **View:** *Contemporary Piano Method DVD*
> Seating and Hand Position (8.06, 9.03)

HAND POSITION

Stand up for a moment and notice that when your arm is by your side in a relaxed manner it falls in a straight line from the elbow to the wrist and that your fingers lie curved.

Sit down once again and bring your arm up onto the keyboard keeping the wrist in the same position and you will have a natural hand position.

(See also Figure 1)

Now place one finger over each of five consecutive notes. Depress all five notes and let the whole weight of the arm rest in the tips of the fingers. Notice how the wrist cannot drop any further when the weight is channelled into the tips of the fingers. The piano is carrying your hand! You do not have to hold your hand above the piano. This is the secret of relaxed playing and good tone.

Next, play the first note with your thumb — let the weight of the arm rest on this note while lifting the second finger high in the air. Now drop the curved second finger on the note, landing on the tip of the finger and transfer the weight into this finger. It should feel like one finger pops up as the next goes down.

Do this with all five fingers up and down a few times. Aim at first for a high, precise finger action. You will find that by lifting each finger up high and dropping, you are using gravity not effort to produce a firm loud tone, a smooth touch (legato) and developing strength in the fingers.

FINDING NOTES ON THE KEYBOARD

For someone who is unfamiliar with the layout of the keyboard, finding the notes quickly and easily can be somewhat of a problem unless it is approached the correct way. The player should be able to **feel** his or her way around the keyboard, so that the eyes are left free to concentrate on the notation. The hands will, however, still be observed from the corner of your eyes and you will need a quick glance now and then, when big leaps occur in the music. The key to feeling one's way around lies in the way the black notes are grouped: in two's and three's.

Place the 2nd and 3rd fingers of the Right Hand on the group of two black notes, and let the thumb fall on the nearest white note. This is 'C'. Do the same with the 2nd, 3rd and 4th fingers on the group of three black notes. The thumb now falls on 'F'. In the Left Hand use fingers 4 and 3 for the two black notes and let the 5th finger fall on 'C', and fingers 4, 3 and 2 for 'F'. As an exercise try to find 'C's and 'F's throughout the length of the keyboard first with eyes open and then with the eyes closed. If Stevie Wonder, Ray Charles and George Shearing can do it, so can you!

Figure 1

Lower Sounds   Higher Sounds

View a demonstration on the CPM *DVD* – Keyboard Location (11.30, 12.54)

Figure 2 – Finger Numbers

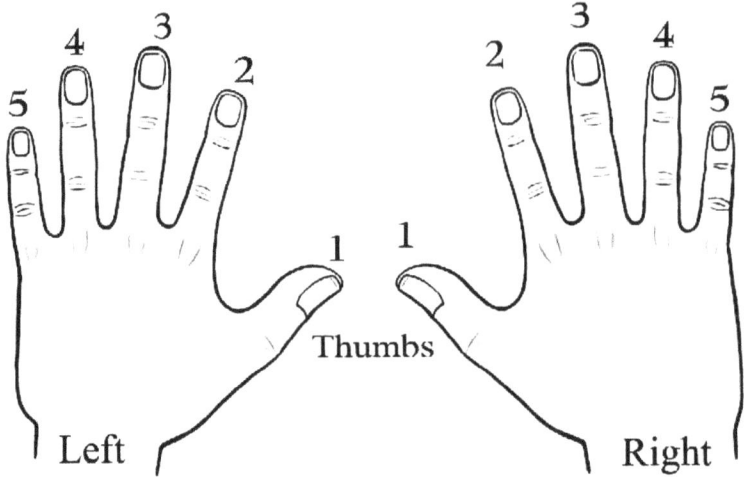

Once you are able to locate the signpost keys (C and F), it is a simple matter to find all the notes –
A B C D E F and G which repeat along the entire length of the keyboard,
producing low, middle range and high sounds.

Contemporary Theory Primer –complete the exercises on keyboard location p4&5.

BEGINNING TO READ

Approach One - The note-naming approach - THE HARD WAY!

Many piano teachers believe the only way to teach reading, is to teach the look of the note on the staff and ask the student to find that note on the keyboard.

What a tedious task having to learn all the names for each note on every line and space, in both bass and treble clefs.

Also, apart from the sheer number of notes to be learnt, playing each note involves four steps:

1) making sure you are reading in the correct clef
2) actually reading each note in isolation by having to memorise rhymes (this is doubly difficult for notes on leger lines for which rhymes are not used)
3) locating the note on the keyboard (by looking down)
4) reading the correct fingering to find the correct finger for each note

This approach usually results in a very halting and disconnected performance, as students look down at the keyboard to find notes (consequently losing their place) and relies a great deal on the process of bar by bar memorisation. Also, as the visual sense is doing all the work, many students do not develop their aural sense, quite often not realising wrong notes are being sounded.

Approach Two - The interval approach - THE EASY WAY!

The other alternative is far more simple and direct:

Find your starting note and from there follow the flow of the music by reading the intervals or distances between the notes.

When players begin with a 'five-finger hand position', intervals of up to a fifth are automatically covered.
- a sixth can be judged from there as a step above or below
- an octave for most people is as far as the hand can comfortably span
- a seventh is one step short of this distance

This approach by its direct correlation of fingers and intervals *eliminates*:
a) having to think about the names of the notes all the time and therefore the confusion between notes on different clefs
b) finding notes on the keyboard (other than the starting note)
c) having to have fingering written in for every note
d) having to look at one's fingers on the keyboard

By following the flow of music, the sense of aural discrimination becomes highly developed. Performers are able to pre-hear the interval then transfer the feeling of the interval to the fingers and use the ear to check that the resulting sound is correct. The approach relies on a balanced combination of the aural, tactile and visual senses.

Look now at page 10 for the easiest way to learn by intervals.

> View a demonstration on the CPM *DVD* – Intervals (20.00)

THE INTERVALS

HOW IT LOOKS **HOW TO PLAY**

Same or unison ⟶ Use same finger twice

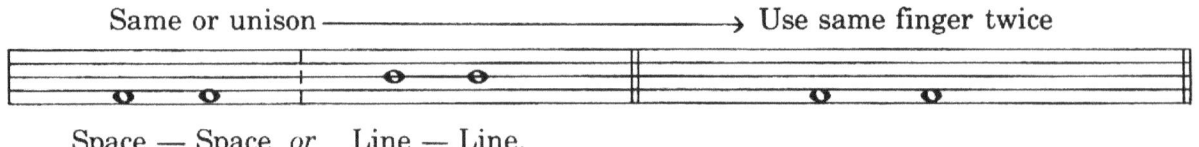

Space — Space *or* Line — Line.

Steps or seconds ⟶ Use one finger per note

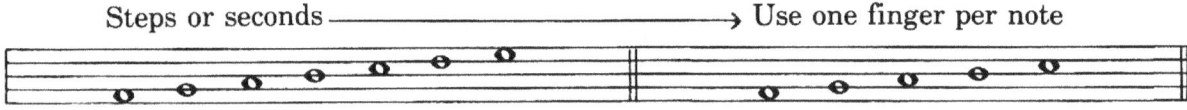

Alternate Lines and Spaces.

Skips or 3rds ⟶ Skip a note/skip one finger

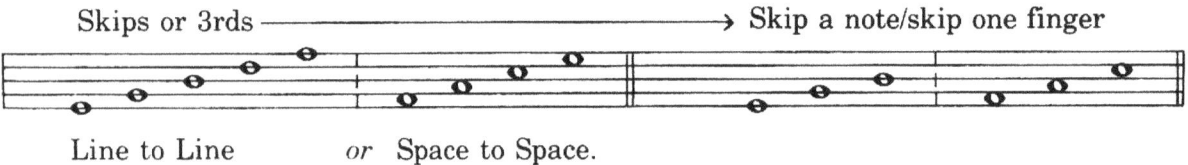

Line to Line *or* Space to Space.

Skip-plus-one or 4th ⟶ Feel a skip and go one further

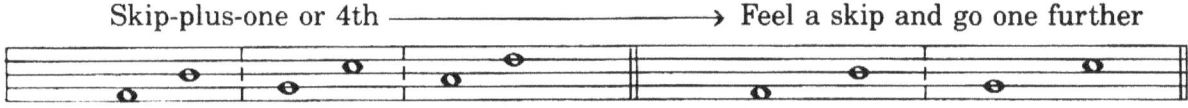

Space to Line *or* vice versa.

Jumps or 5ths ⟶ Feels like 2 skips

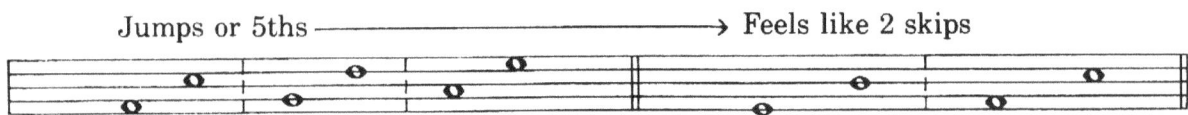

Space to Space *or* Line to Line.

Play all of these intervals in different areas of the keyboard in order to establish their feel and the sound.
Play them both melodically (one after the other) and harmonically (both notes sounding at one time).
Teachers: play the interval drill game with students.

> Listen to interval sounds in the *Contemporary Aural Course* – Preparatory Set and Set One

> View a demonstration of interval writing on the CPM *DVD* – Intervals (20.00)

Write some repeated notes (**same**) next to the given notes.

e.g. same

Write some **steps** going **up** from the given notes.

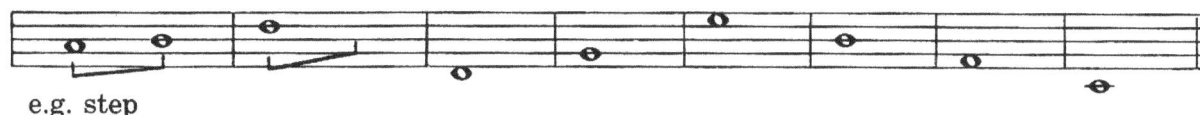

e.g. step

Write some **steps** going **down** from the given notes.

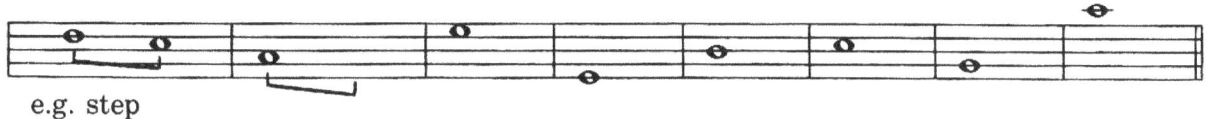

e.g. step

Write **skips up**.   Write **skips down**.

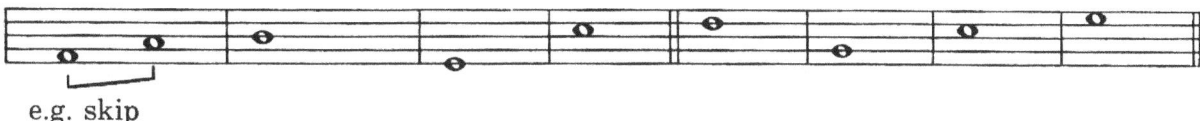

e.g. skip

Write '**skip-plus-1's**' up.   Write '**skip-plus-1's**' down.

e.g. skip + 1

Write **jumps up**.   Write **jumps down**.

e.g. jump

> Learn the basics of staff notation & practice reading and writing intervals:
> - *Contemporary Theory Primer* p6-11, 18-19
> - *Contemporary Theory Workbook* – Bk 1, p5-11

SOME VERY USEFUL INFORMATION

If you are seated correctly at the centre of the keyboard, middle 'C' should be approximately opposite your navel. It is also called middle 'C' because it is written in the middle of the Great Staff (the two sets of five lines used for piano music).

Colour Coding instructions for all the Signpost C's used in this book are available from
www.margaretbrandman.com

THE GREAT STAFF

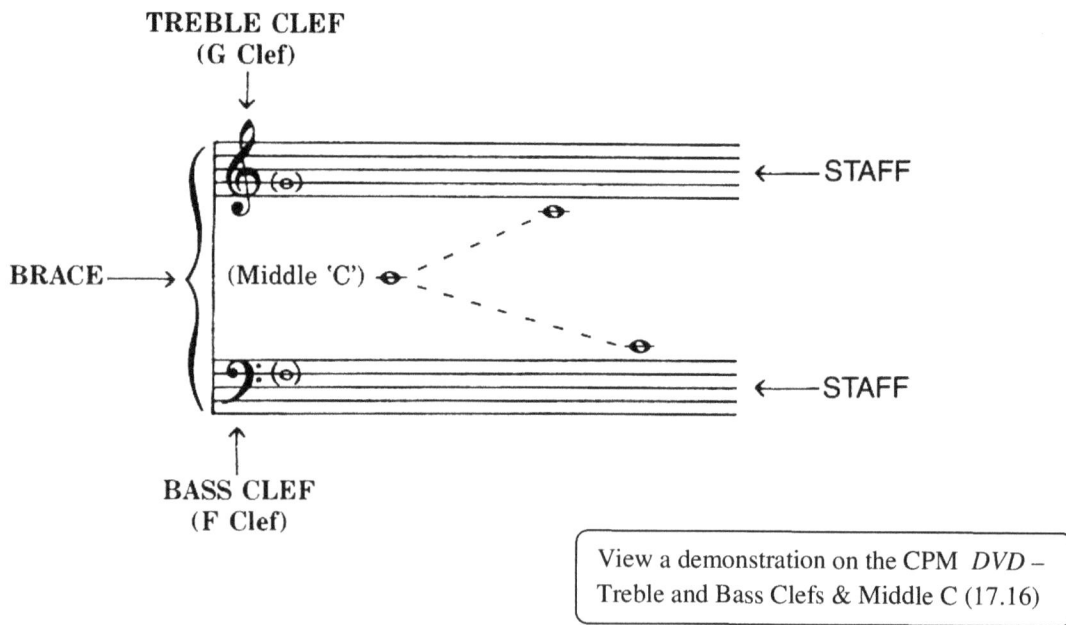

View a demonstration on the CPM *DVD* –
Treble and Bass Clefs & Middle C (17.16)

The Treble Clef (𝄞) usually indicates that the Right Hand plays the notes on its staff. It is also known as the 'G' Clef. The curl in the middle starts on the line that the note G is written on.

The Bass Clef (𝄢) usually indicates that the Left Hand plays the notes on its staff. It is also known as the 'F' Clef. The two dots surround the line that F is written on.

Learn to write treble and bass clefs and the signpost C's:
- *Contemporary Theory Primer* p16-17
- *Contemporary Theory Workbook* – Bk 1, p12-16

TIME VALUES OF NOTES AND RESTS

In music we use **notes** to indicate **sounds** and **rests** to indicate periods of **silence**.

NOTES

o	— Whole note	also known as a Semibreve	— 4 counts
𝅗𝅥	— Half note	also known as a Minim	— 2 counts
♩	— Quarter note	also known as Crotchet	— 1 count
♪	— Eighth Note	also known as a Quaver	— ½ count
𝅘𝅥𝅯	— Sixteenth note	also known as a Semiquaver	— ¼ count

RESTS

𝄻	— Whole rest	— Semibreve rest	— 4 counts
𝄼	— Half rest	— Minim rest	— 2 counts
𝄽	— Quarter rest	— Crotchet rest	— 1 count
𝄾	— Eighth rest	— Quaver rest	— ½ count
𝄿	— Sixteenth rest	— Semiquaver rest	— ¼ count

> View a demonstration on the CPM *DVD* – Rhythm (28.16)

> Learn about rhythm notation using the CPM's unique colour-coding system then clap the rhythms:
> - *Contemporary Theory Primer* p12-15 and *Contemporary Theory Workbook* – Bk 1, p20-22

HOW TO PLAY THE MUSIC ON THE FOLLOWING PAGES

Each of the lines of music is in 4/4 time, which means that each bar or measure contains four quarter notes (four blues or their equivalent value notes). Play each line of music slowly and evenly. Most students find it helpful to say aloud the **interval distance and direction** as they play. If possible they should be encouraged to pitch the sounds. This helps train voice, ear, eye and hand. When a repeated note is written, lift the finger to play the note again and say 'Same' as you play the note a second time. When a rest appears, lift the finger off the key (quit the key). Also quit the key cleanly at the end of each line of music where the word 'off' is written.

There are two ways to talk/sing this music as you play.

For beginning students:
  1) Say the intervals and direction in place of the number you would usually count.
      For example: One   2   step up   2 | step up   2   step down   2 | step down   2   3   4 | off

For more experienced students:
  2) Say the intervals and counting, making sure that the direction is observed.
      For example: One   2   3   4 | st   2   sk   2 | st   st   st   sk | sk   2   3   4 | off

INTERVAL EXERCISES. Hand Position 1.
(Start on Middle C)
RIGHT HAND PLAYS

When notes move *up* on the page, they move to the **right** on the piano keyboard, producing higher sounds.

When notes move *down* on the page, they move to the **left** on the piano keyboard, producing lower sounds.

Say the distance and direction when you see this sign (*). For example Step Up or Skip Down

HAND POSITION I.

The vertical lines are BAR LINES

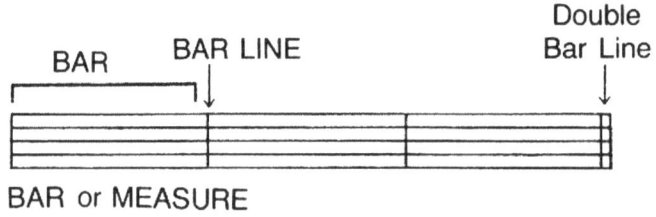

The areas between the bar lines are known as bars or measures.

At the end of a section a **Double Bar Line** is used.

View a demonstration on the CPM *DVD* – Putting it All Together (33.29)

INTERVAL EXERCISES. Hand Position 2.

Say intervals and count aloud as you play. If you find **'skip-plus-one'**, a little difficult to say shorten the phrase to **'plus-one'**, always keeping in mind that it **means** skip-plus-one.

LEFT HAND PLAYS.

Start with thumb on middle C.

HAND POSITION 2.

- Always listen to what you are playing. Try to **hear** what a step sounds like, and get to know what it **feels** like. Do the same with the skips, skip + 1's, and jumps.
- Leave your **eyes** free to follow the notes on the page. Do not disturb their concentration by looking down at your hands. If you feel tempted, ask a friend to hold a book above your hands as a barrier, for a short while.
  This way you will train yourself to feel and hear the intervals.

- Any of the following interval exercises, can be played, hands together, provided that the starting notes are 8 notes (an octave) apart. In other words, both hands starting on notes with the same letter name. Playing the exercises in this manner, helps build strength and co-ordination in the hands.

ADVANCED PLAYERS' EXERCISES

Make each note equal in length. Play slowly and surely. Say distances out aloud.

(1) Do not begin on 'E' or 'G'. Think about the distances only — not the note names!

(2) Do not begin on 'F' or 'A'

You will find this system transfers easily to the leger lines.
(The extra lines used to extend the staff).

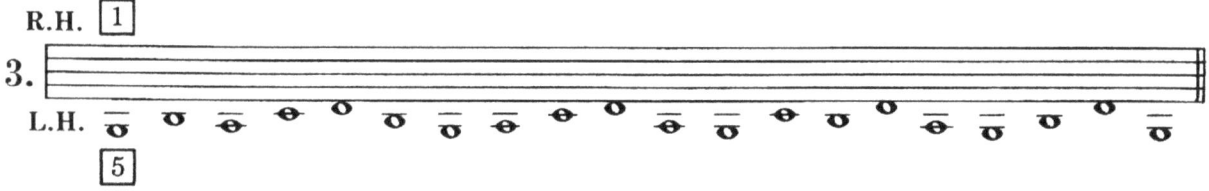

(3) Do not begin on 'G' or 'B'.

If you prefer to, say 2nd, 3rd, 4th and 5th instead of step, skip etc.

INSTANT TRANSPOSITION

If you have read music by the note names previously, disregard the Clef signs (cover them up if you wish) and the names of the notes in the following pages, up to the section where the pieces are written with key signatures. Begin each exercise and piece in a different area of the keyboard and make sure you are reading intervals only! Play some of the exercises with both hands starting an octave apart.

017
HAND POSITIONS 3 and 4

These pages contain reading exercises in two new hand positions, using the intervals up to 'jump' or 'fifth'. Once you are familiar with at least the sign-post notes of the first four positions there will be many pieces you can start to play. Begin with the tunes in *Dexter's Easy Piano Pieces*.

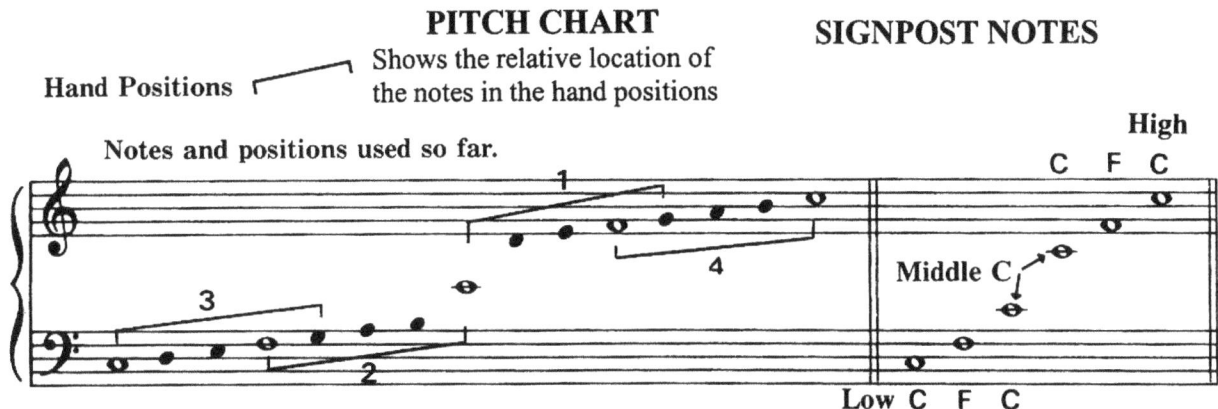

Colour Code the Signpost C's in this Pitch Chart

Something Extra

- Colour and clap page five of *Daily Dexter-Flexers*, then add the 'ands' (+) into the counting, for the music given below. For example: **1 + 2 + Skip + 2 +** , or **1 + Step + Step + Skip +**
- Skill building: for two-handed reading practice using steps and focussing on direction play Group One from *Daily Dexter-Flexers*.

View a demonstration on the CPM *DVD* – Signpost C's (34.15)

EXERCISES USING REPEATED NOTES IN HAND POSITIONS 3 & 4

Add the 'and' into the talk through, to allow for a lift of the finger before a repeated note. Play all the other intervals smoothly and connected (legato). Say: One + Same + Step + Same + and so on.

HAND POSITION 3

1 Same Step ✻ ✻ ✻ ✻ ✻ ✻ ✻ ✻ ✻ ✻ ✻ ✻ ✻ Step 2 off

HAND POSITION 4

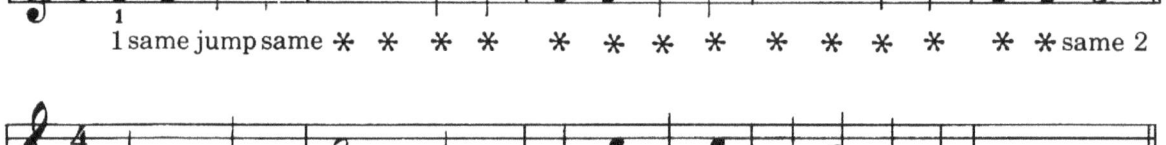

1 same jump same ✻ ✻ ✻ ✻ ✻ ✻ ✻ ✻ ✻ ✻ ✻ ✻ ✻ same 2

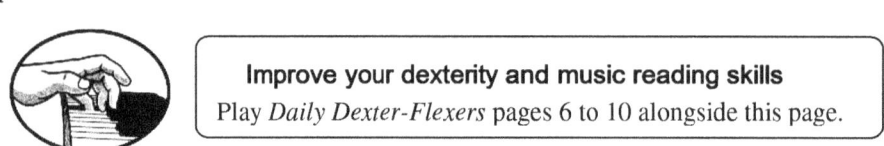

Improve your dexterity and music reading skills
Play *Daily Dexter-Flexers* pages 6 to 10 alongside this page.

PLAYING WITH TWO HANDS TOGETHER

I recommend doing pieces together at an early stage as this avoids the mental block many people develop when they start on 'Beginners' books, especially those with large notes. Figure 1 is an example of the type of piece presented in these books. Note how the sense of reading and feeling the distances is disturbed by the melody jumping from one hand to the other. Also the hands do not learn to co-ordinate, as at no time do they actually play together.

<u>DO NOT PLAY</u>

Figure 1
THE WRONG WAY

DOUBLE HAND POSITIONS (H.P.)

After you have played No. 1 separately, try to put it together, even in your first practice session. You will find it very easy as both hands are doing the same thing.

When reading two hands together always focus your eyes on the **LOWER** of the two staves. Your eyes can easily take in material **ABOVE** the point of focus. They **cannot** take in material below the point of focus.

Also the foundation of the piece is in the bass, so it is wise to build up from there, especially when reading **chords** which we will be coming to shortly.

Improve your dexterity and music reading skills
Play *Dexter's Easy Piano Pieces* pages 7-8 alongside this page.

Integrated Theory and Ear-training for Complete Study

Theory

Contemporary Theory Primer:
- The basics of staff notation, signpost notes, interval writing and recognition, plus practical rhythm training with rhythm boxes to colour and clap.

Contemporary Theory Workbook: Books 1 & 2
- General theory: intervals, clefs, note-names and intervals combined, rhythm, scale construction, chord construction and more...

Ear-Training

Contemporary Aural Course –Audio and workbooks with answer sheets.
- Preparatory Level and Sets 1 and 2. Refer to the website for details.

SUGGESTED COMPLEMENTARY BOOK

Another excellent book to use is the 'Counting Time' book by Scott O'Neal published by Alfred Music. This book is a very valuable aid to visualising time values and learning to sight read. As each note is written in correct proportion and given the appropriate amount of space on the page, the eye is able to move along the line at an even rate and confusions of timing which occur in a great deal of printed music are eliminated.

Each bar of notes is placed above boxes of equal length which have been subdivided so that the pulse can be seen.

For example:

The author suggests cross hatching the boxes in lead pencil. However I find that using a series of matched colours produces a far more vivid and clear picture. The rests are left blank and therefore stand out very sharply on the page. Students learn that rests are just as important, **not** as the name suggests 'a place to go to sleep!'

The colour system I use is:

𝅝	= mauve and purple	♪	= red and pink
𝅗𝅥	= yellow and orange	♫	= dark green and light green
♩	= dark blue and light blue	♬	= brown and black

The sets of colours are designed so that each new note to be struck receives a contrasting colour. When clapping, keep the hands together as long as the colour continues, and take them apart for rests.

After the exercises have been coloured in, it is advisable to clap them through from left to right across the page. This also gives experience in reading changing time signatures.

A similar system of diagrams to display the timing is employed in this volume. Colour the boxes in the suggested colour scheme and clap the timing before playing each piece.

The **Time Signature** (sign) is made up of the two numbers at the beginning of the music. The **top** number tells **how many** counts in the bar and the **lower** number tells what **kind of note** (¼ ⅛ 1/16) etc. receives one count.

COLOUR INSTRUCTIONS

Colour:	semibreve	mauve	Colour:	1st crotchet	dark blue
"	1st minim	yellow	"	2nd crotchet	light blue
"	2nd minim	orange	"	3rd crotchet	dark blue
			"	4th crotchet	light blue

COLOUR AND CLAP THIS LINE   **COUNT OUT LOUD**

PLAYING TUNES WITH VARYING INTERVALS BETWEEN THE HANDS

To play the following tunes with hands together follow this procedure:
1) Find the starting note for each hand, sound it and hold it down.
2) Read the **left hand** distance (e.g. step up or skip down) and prepare it, by poising the finger in the air. You can even move the finger up and down, without sounding the note, to connect the visual message with the feeling in the finger.
3) Read the **right hand** distance and prepare to play it.
4) When ready, play both intervals with two hands at the same time.

The first few times you play with hands together, it is useful to play very slowly and say the intervals aloud. For instance (left hand) 'step' and (right hand) 'jump'.

- Continue by completing moves 2, 3 and 4 till the end of the piece.
- If a note has two or more counts, say the counts after the intervals, using the time to do the preparation for 2 and 3.

In this next piece, you can say 'back in' when the two thumbs play 'middle C'. Once you can read the intervals silently, say the **direction** while adding the 'and' count to help co-ordination.
For instance: 1 + out + in + out +

1. MOVIN' AROUND

Colour: 1st crotchet — dark blue
          2nd crotchet — light blue   etc.
          semibreve   — mauve

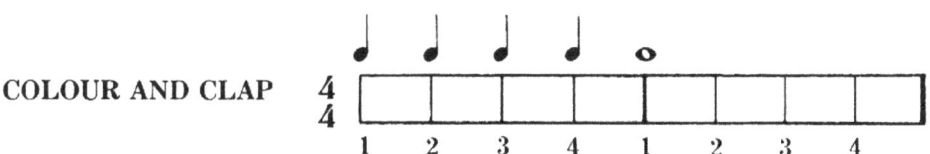

COLOUR AND CLAP

The usual practice procedure is to play hands separately before playing together.

H.P. 1   **PLAY SLOWLY AND EVENLY**

H.P. 2

2. FEELIN' THE KEYS

Expand your repertoire
Apply the new skills learned on these pages to *Junior Trax* p5-**7**

Colour: 1st minim — yellow
2nd minim — orange etc.
Colour crotchets as before

COLOUR AND CLAP

- Cuing - *refer to Guide Notes on page 65*

 **Improve your dexterity**: Play *Daily Dexter-Flexers* p11-12 alongside this page.

When playing both hands together, always look for the SHAPES created by the movement of the INTERVALS in each hand.

The two hands may move UP together ∕═ or DOWN together ═∖

OR The two hands may move OUTWARDS ═< or INWARDS >═

OR in an **oblique** fashion (where one stays and the other moves).

OR both may stay on the same note. ═══

3. FINGER PLAY

COLOUR AND CLAP

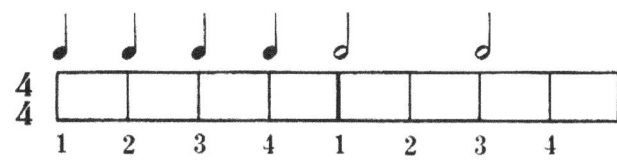

Expand your repertoire
Apply your new skills to *Junior Trax* p8-9 and *Dexter's Easy Piano Pieces* p9

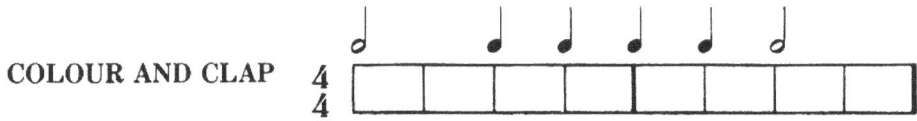

Prepare for this piece: play *Daily Dexter-Flexers* p13 before playing No3 with hands together.

4. DOIN' THE STEP-SKIP RAG

COLOUR AND CLAP

Look for the mixtures of intervals between the treble and bass lines. Listen for the sounds. Are they dissonant (clashy) or consonant (pleasant)?

HAND POSITIONS 5 and 6.

Here are two more hand positions using the intervals up to a fifth (jump). Figure 1 is a chart of the range and relative position of the sign-post notes and Hand Positions learned so far.

Figure 1

PITCH CHART

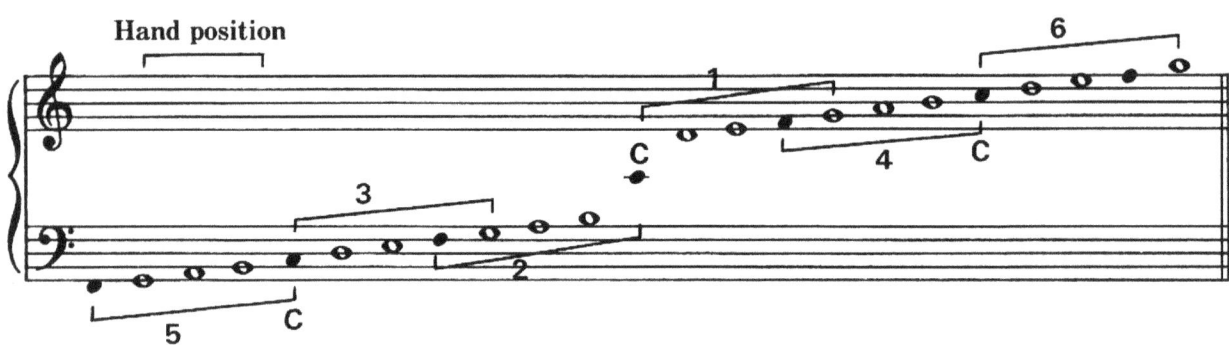

HAND POSITION 5

HAND POSITION 6

5. MOVIN' DOWN THE LINE

COLOUR AND CLAP
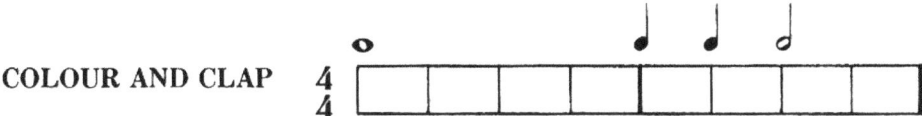

 **Prepare for this piece:** play *Daily Dexter-Flexers* p14-17.

Expand your repertoire: apply the new skills learned on these pages
to the pieces in *Junior Trax* p8-9 and *Dexter's Easy Piano Pieces* p10.

C AND G MAJOR SCALES

Now that hand positions 1 to 5 have been learnt we can move on to the scales of C and G Major. A scale is simply a ladder of notes usually covering at least one octave in range. (Oct = 8 therefore an octave = the distance between two notes, eight notes from each other.)

The scale fingering for most of the scales that begin on the white notes is a combination of **two hand positions**. As you have only five fingers and have to cover eight notes, use the hand position for five notes and three fingers for the remainder (See Figure 1). When playing the Right Hand ascending, use the set of three fingers first, then by passing the thumb **under** the third finger the hand position notes can be played. My sign for thumb under is ⤵. When playing the scale descending the reverse happens and the third finger must go **over** the thumb at the same spot. My sign for the third finger over is ⤴. The Left Hand of course will do the same thing in mirror image. Learn the fingering for C major well as it applies also to G, D, A and E scales.

C MAJOR SCALE

Figure 1

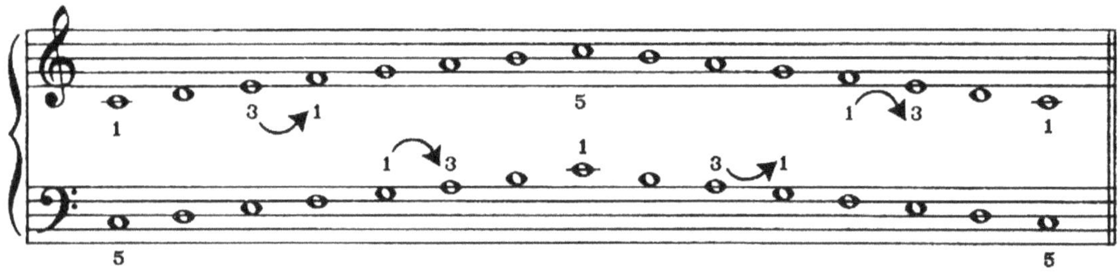

Practise separate hands first, then hands together

Refer to: • Pictorial Patterns for Keyboard Scales and Chords

SHARP (♯), FLAT (♭) AND NATURAL (♮)

The sign used when a note has to be raised a semitone is a Sharp (♯). If the note is to be lowered a semitone a Flat is used (♭). If either of these has to be cancelled, a Natural sign is used (♮). The Natural brings the note back to the ordinary white note on the keyboard. Collectively these signs are called Accidentals.

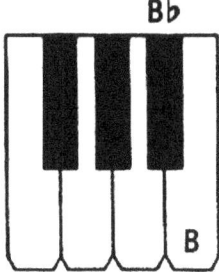

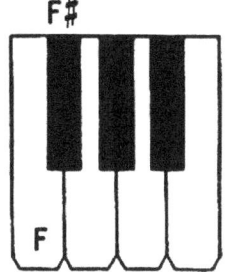

A *flattened* note is played on the very next key to the *left*.

A *sharpened* note is played on the very next key to the *right*.

The effect of an accidental lasts until the end of the bar and the bar line acts as an eraser. In other words the sharp, flat or natural used as an Accidental affects all the notes within one bar which are written on exactly the same position on the staff. Thus if the sharp were written in front of a note on the second line in the Treble Staff, all the notes on the second line (on that staff only) would be sharpened until the end of the bar.

However, if the sharp or flat belongs to the Scale, it will be written at the beginning of each line as a Key Signature. You must then play all the notes with the same name as those at the beginning of the line, sharp or flat as the case may be.

Expand your repertoire
Play these pieces which include accidentals:
Junior Trax p22
Hot Trax p8-10.

For more practice with **accidentals** complete pages 26-31 in *Contemporary Theory Workbook* Bk.1.

TONES AND SEMITONES

Before moving on to other major scales, one should know how a major scale is constructed. If major scales starting on different notes are to have the same sound, they must all have the same arrangement of tones and semitones. (This also accounts for the varying amount of black notes in the different scales.) Let us look at tones and semitones and then at C major scale as our pattern.

Apart from what we already know as steps between the notes, there are also two different types of steps: Half Steps or Semitones (S) and Whole Steps or Tones (T).

A Semitone is the distance from one note to the very next nearest, be it black or white. For example:

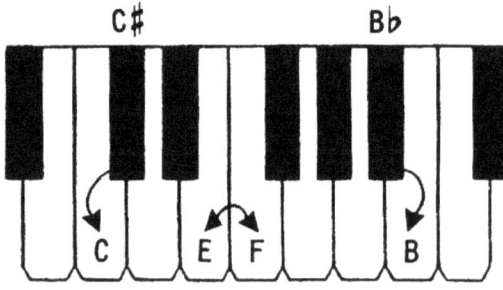

A Tone is therefore twice this distance. In other words miss out one key only. For example:

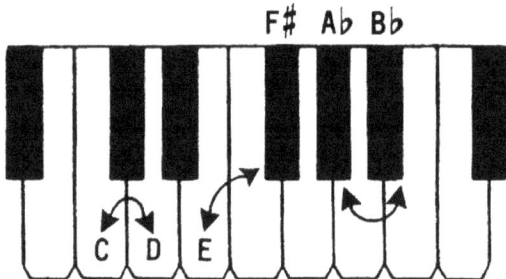

Thus you can clearly see that C major has the distances T T S T T T S. (See Figure 1).

Figure 1 C MAJOR SCALE

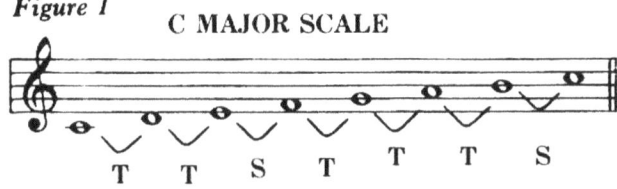

Build G scale on the keyboard using fingers 5 4 3 2 (LH) and 2 3 4 5 (RH). Find the tones and semitones in the same order as the pattern for C Major scale, holding down the notes so that you can see the entire pattern blocked out on the keyboard. If you follow the pattern correctly, the second last note will be a black key - F sharp. (See page 67 for the pictorial pattern)

Figure 2 G MAJOR SCALE

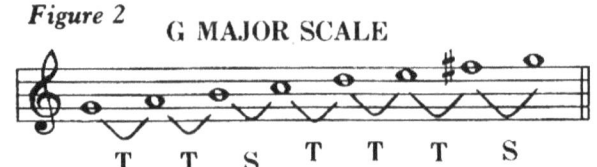

Now play the G Major Scale ascending and descending, separate hands first, and then hands together.

C MAJOR CONTRARY MOTION SCALE

Practise C and G scales separately and then hands together in similar motion, (both hands moving in the same direction), in the form given on page 26. Then try C Major in Contrary Motion. See Figure 1. You will find this easy as both hands are doing the same thing at the same time. When playing Contrary Motion scales, always practise the Right Hand ascending (↑) and descending (↓) first, then the Left Hand descending (↓) and ascending (↑) and then play two hands together.

Figure 1

C MAJOR CONTRARY MOTION

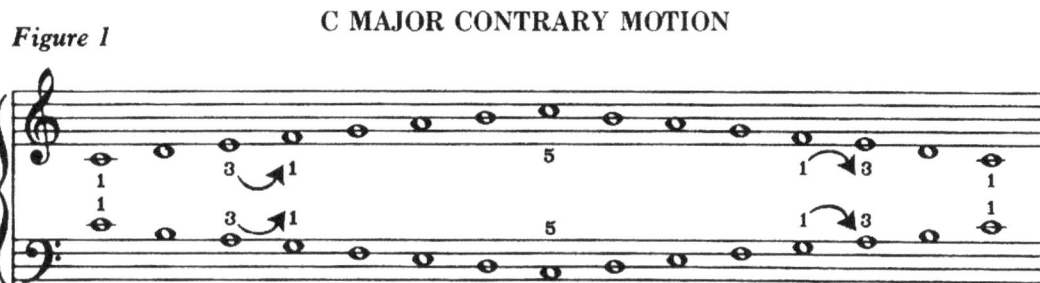

Expand your repertoire: apply the new skills learned on this page to the pieces in *Junior Trax* p11 and *Dexter's Easy Piano Pieces* p11&12

6. SWINGING ALONG

A dot after a note extends the note by half of the original value of the note.

e.g. 𝅗𝅥. — 2 counts plus the dot (1 count) = 3 counts.

WHEN YOU SEE A DOT, STRETCH THE COLOUR FOR THE EXTRA BOX.

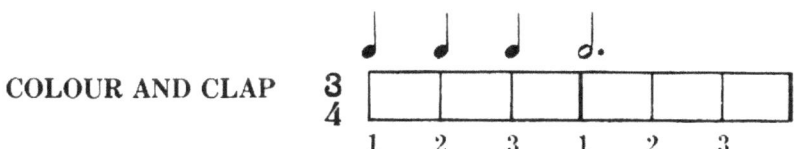

COLOUR AND CLAP

HAND POSITIONS 7 AND 8

The two new hand positions, extending to very low C and very high C are shown below.

The short lines drawn above and below the staff are known as Leger lines.

HAND POSITION 7

HAND POSITION 8

The total range of notes used up to now is shown in Figure 1.

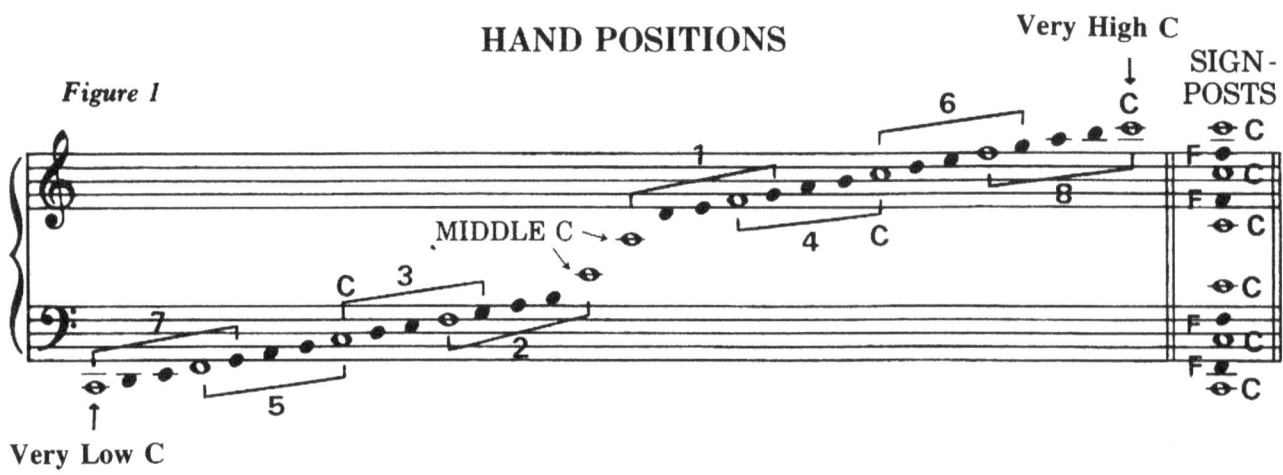

Colour Code the Signpost C's in Figure 1.

7. TIRED FEET

Direction Concepts
Refer to guide notes on p 65

COLOUR AND CLAP

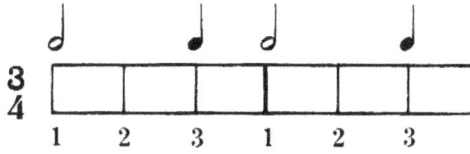

Expand your repertoire
Play *Junior Trax* p14 and
*Dexter's Easy
Piano Pieces* p14&15

8. SINGIN' HIGH

COLOUR AND CLAP

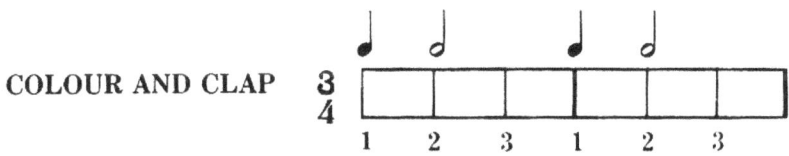

DEGREE NAMES AND NUMBERS

- When scales are written, each note in the scale can be given a number from one to eight.

- The numbers are known as Scale Degree Numbers.

- The degree numbers are usually written in Roman Numerals as follows:

I	II	III	IV	V	VI	VII	VIII
(1)	(2)	(3)	(4)	(5)	(6)	(7)	(8)

- Each of the notes of the scales can also be given a DEGREE NAME or Technical Name, which tells us something about the function of that note in relation to the scale.

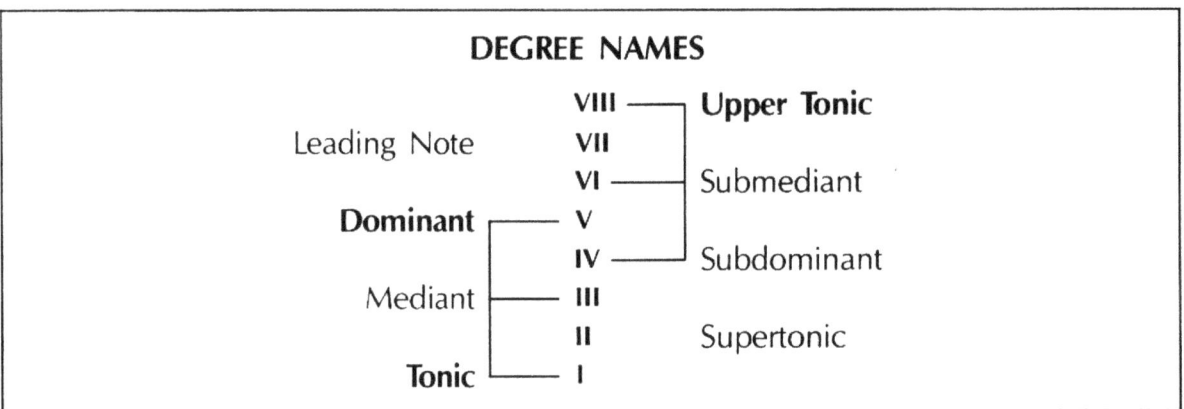

MEANINGS OF THE TECHNICAL DEGREE NAMES

- **Tonic (I)** - The first degree is called the Tonic, meaning 'keynote' of the scale.

- **Upper Tonic (VIII)** - This is the last note of the scale. It has the same name as the Tonic and is found an octave above it.

- **Dominant (V)** - This is the fifth degree above the Tonic and the *most important* note in relation to the Tonic. Most pieces move to the Dominant as a point of rest in the middle.

- **Subdominant (IV)** - Although this note is the fourth note of the scale, its function is as the *most important note below* the Upper Tonic. It is found a jump or fifth *below* the Upper Tonic. For this reason it is known as the Subdominant (*sub* means 'below' or 'under'). It is the next most important point of rest in a piece of music.

- **Mediant (III)** - The word *mediant* means 'midway'. The Mediant degree is midway between the Tonic and the Dominant.

- **Submediant (VI)** - The middle note between the Subdominant and the Upper Tonic.

- **Supertonic (II)** - *Super* means 'above', or 'more than' or 'bigger than'. This degree is located just above the Tonic.

- **Leading Note (VII)** - This degree is also known as the *leading tone* because of its function of leading the sound on to the Upper Tonic note of the scale.

The Major Chord

• To find the Major Chord from the Major scale take the Tonic (I), Mediant (III) and Dominant (V) notes and play them at the same time. This is called the Root position. (See Figure 1). **Another way** of finding the Chord is to build it up from the Tonic by **counting the semitones.** Between the Tonic and the Mediant there are 4 semitones, and between the Mediant and the Dominant there are three semitones.

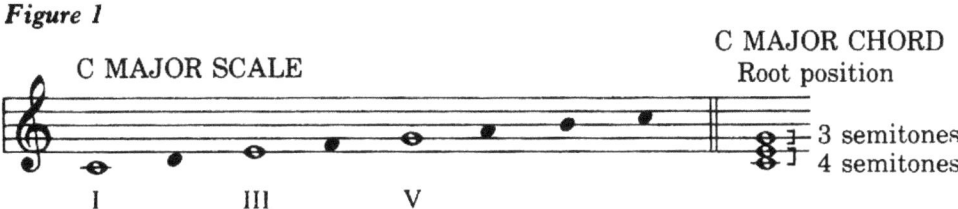

• All chords should be also learnt in **inversions. To invert** means **to turn upside down,** therefore the same notes are played in different arrangements, so that the lowest note in one inversion becomes the highest note in the next.

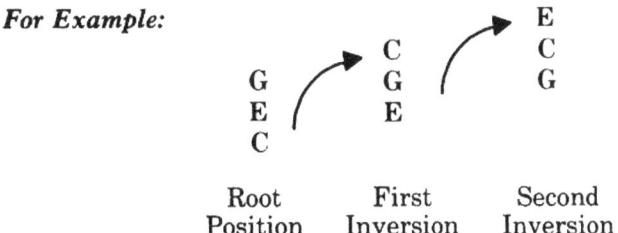

See Figure 2. This is a suggested way to practise three-note chords and inversions.

You will notice that 2 notes of the first chord are the same in the second chord.

• A good way to begin playing inversions, is to swap fingers onto the two notes that are the same, without lifting off the keyboard. That leaves only one new note, (the one that is being moved from its position at the bottom of the chord) to be transferred to the top of the next inversion.

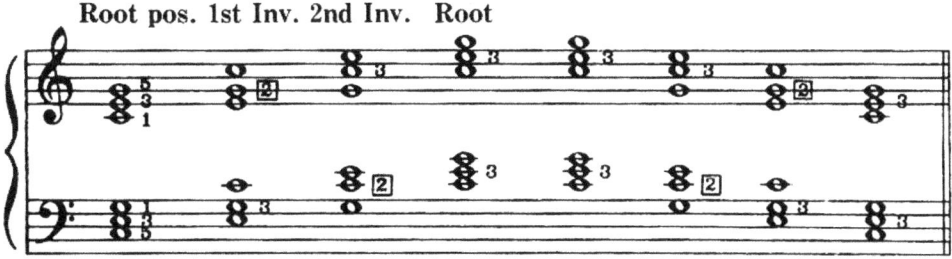

Use 1st & 5th fingers on the outside notes of each inversion.

• As soon as a scale is learnt, practise also its chord and inversion. This way you will become familiar with all keys very quickly and no one key will be harder than any other. Use the same inversion fingering for all three-note chords even if the thumb lands on a black note. Though thumbs on black notes are avoided in scales, they are necessary and natural in chord fingering.

Here is an arrangement of a tune which is also a popular **round** that dates back to 1609.

The Right Hand melody can be played or sung by 2 or more people starting one, two, three or four bars apart.

9. DERRY DING DING DASON

* Derry is sung on the first crotchet.

* Derry Ding Ding | Dason
I am John | Cheston, We
Weed-on we | wod-en we
Weed-on we | wod-en Bim
Bom bim | Bom Bim | Bom.

Fermata

♩ or ♩
Pause Sign
Hold for longer than written value

Arranged by
M. S. BRANDMAN

CROSS-OVER POSITIONS

If you concentrate on the intervals, exercises on leger lines should be just as easy to read as those on the staff.

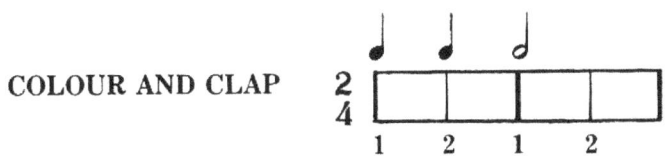

Expand your repertoire: play *Junior Trax* p16 and *Hot Trax* p4-7

PLAY C SCALE AND C CHORD THEN PLAY NO. 10

10. KEEP ON SKIPPIN'

Tie
From one note to the same note. It has
the effect of combining the note values.
(Do not strike the 2nd note).

e.g.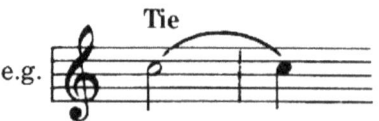

PLAY G SCALE AND G CHORD THEN PLAY NO. 11.

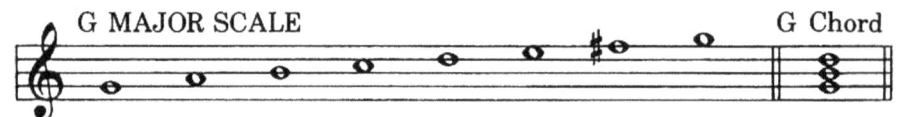

11. TIE ONE ON

COLOUR AND CLAP

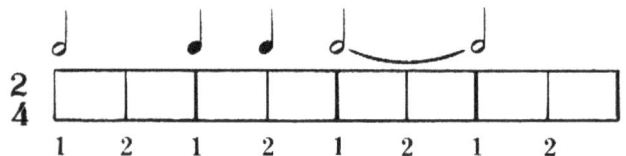

STRETCH THE COLOUR
OVER 4 BOXES
FOR THE TIED NOTES.

KEY G

Expand your repertoire and chord skills: play *It's Easy to Improvise pp 6, 7 &12*

Expand your repertoire in the key of G major: *Junior Trax p12-13 & p15*
Dexter's Easy Piano Pieces p11&13 ; Christmas Favourites p5

Repeat signs

The usual way of indicating a repeat is to place double dots at the beginning and end of a section. These are found in the second and third spaces of the staff above one another.

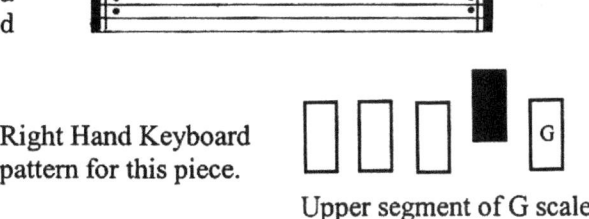

Right Hand Keyboard pattern for this piece.

Upper segment of G scale

12. PROMENADING

Before playing any piece, play the scale and chord of the key. Then find the segment of scale that is being used in the music and place your fingers over the pattern of black and white notes before commencing to play. Continue to read by intervals while maintaining the keyboard pattern for the key.

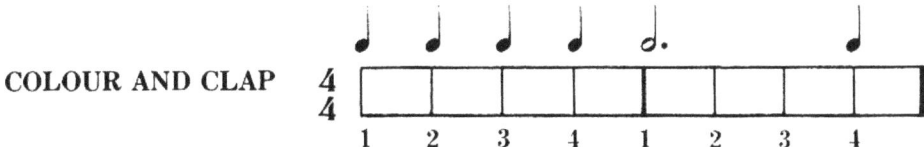

PLAY THE WHOLE PIECE TWICE

*** *For more experience playing in the key of G Major, transpose the first two pieces in this book to G Major (see pp 21 & 22). In these pieces you will find that the Left Hand is set on the **upper** notes of G scale, while the Right Hand plays only the **lower** five white notes.*

HINTS ON THE ECONOMICAL USE OF PRACTICE TIME

If a small section of the piece is giving you trouble, do not play through from the beginning each time to fix it.

Extract the problem area, whether it be two, three or four notes, and repeat the section a few times. When the section is comfortable to play, and the fingers are managing easily, play through the piece from the beginning and you will find that the section no longer presents a problem.

MAJOR SCALES - D, A and E

- If we apply the Major Scale pattern discussed on page 28 to D, A and E, we find that D Major scale has 2 sharps - F sharp and C sharp; A Major scale has 3 sharps - F sharp, C sharp and G sharp; and E Major scale has 4 sharps - F sharp, C sharp, G sharp and D sharp. Notice that the sharps from the previous scale are retained as the new sharp is added to the order. The new sharp is always the second last note of the scale. You will find it helpful to learn the sharps in this order as this is the way they are grouped in the Key Signature at the beginning of each line of music (see page 39). After a while you will be able to tell at a glance how many sharps or flats are in the Key Signature and therefore what scale or key the music is in.

Figure 1

- These three scales have the same fingering as C Major. Before starting a new scale, find the pattern of black and white notes on the keyboard. Hold down all 8 white notes for one octave of the piano using fingers 5 4 3 2 (LH) and 2 3 4 5 (RH). Then shift the fingers for the required sharps (in key signature order) onto the black keys so that the total picture of the scale can be seen. You will find it easier to learn and remember a scale by its keyboard pattern than by reading it.

**Keyboard Pattern for
A Major Scale**

Figure 2

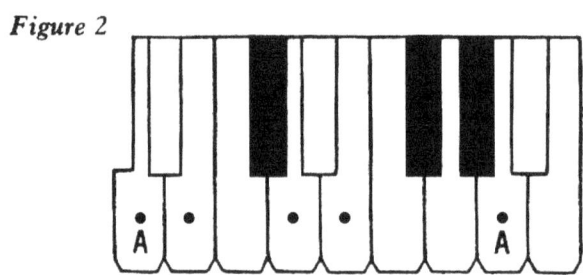

- Play D, A and E Major scales in the form given for C Major on p 26. Some students may like to learn one scale per week, others may find it easy to learn all three scales at the same time. Also play the matching major chords of each key by taking the first, third and fifth notes of each scale and sounding them together. When the scales are secure in Similar Motion, play them in Contrary Motion according to the manner described on page 29.

KEY SIGNATURES

KEY FACTS!

1) The tonic note for each of the above keys is a jump or fifth *higher* than the previous scale.

2) The Key Signature sharps always follow this order: F C G D A E B
   Here is an easy rhyme to help you remember them in order:

   Fast Cars Go Down At Every Bend

The keys on this page use only the first four sharps from the sequence. Practice these scales in rising key signature order, that is: around the cycle of fifths. See the keyboard patterns on page 67.

Refer to: • Pictorial Patterns for Keyboard Scales and Chords

SIXTHS

The interval (distance) of a Sixth is one step further than a 'jump' (or 5th). Stretch the fifth finger or the thumb one note beyond the Hand Position to reach it. Notice that the sixth looks similar to a Step or a 'Skip-plus-one'. It is always written from a line note to a space note or vice-versa.

These exercises can be played with either hand, separately or together. There is no fixed starting note. Begin on any note you wish.

> **Learn to write and recognise the larger intervals:**
> *Contemporary Theory Primer* - pages 32-36
> *Contemporary Theory Workbook* – Book 1, pages 42-44

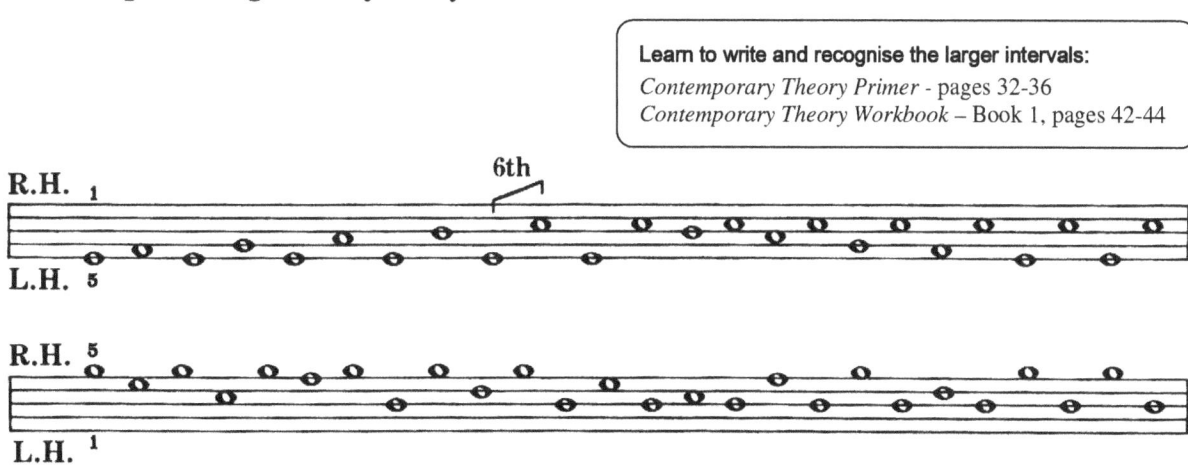

> **Improve your dexterity using sixths:** play *Daily Dexter-Flexers* p19-20
> **Improve your key practice:** *transpose Daily Dexter-Flexers* p7-18 to each new key
> **Expand your repertoire using sixths:** play *Dexter's Easy Piano Pieces* p16&17
> and *It's Easy to Improvise* p13&14

PRIMARY CHORDS

In a simple piece of music or a blues pattern, a basic structure of chords is used. The Melody usually outlines the notes of the chord and uses notes of the scale in between. If the left hand is playing an accompaniment it usually plays two or more notes of the chord under the right hand melody. This basic chord structure is made up from the **primary** (or most important) chords which are built on notes of the scale. Three-note chords or "Triads" can be built on every note of the scale, but the most important ones are built on the Tonic (1), Subdominant (4) and Dominant (5) notes of the scale. See Figure 1.

When you learn a piece of music, find out what these three important chords are in the key of the piece concerned, and then try to spot them on the music. If you know what to expect there will be less likelihood of playing the wrong note. If you see a chord in a strange position you will also be able to make an **educated** guess as to what it should be.

To help you in this spotting procedure, I suggest writing a **table of chords** in a blank area on the page. **The table should look like this: IV I V.** When the chords are set out in this manner they can easily be seen as part of the Circle of Fifths. (See page 63). Thus in C major, the table of chords would be:

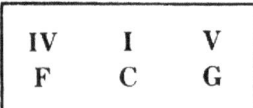

The single-letter name implies the whole chord. It is standard procedure in popular music to write only the letter-name for a **major** chord. (For minor chords a small m or mi follows the letter name).

Place the thumbs of both hands on Middle C, then locate the Dominant degree (G) a jump or fifth above the Tonic in the right hand and the Subdominant degree (F) a jump or fifth below the tonic in the left hand.

Figure 1

**PRIMARY TRIADS
I, IV & V**

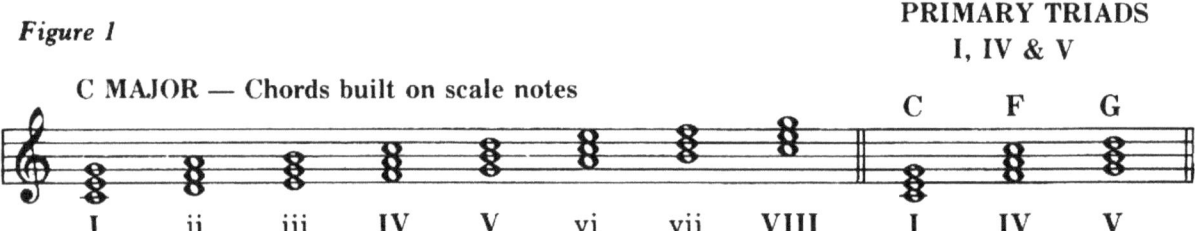

In Figure 2 I have given an example of a piece of music and how to find the chords, using the Table as a guide to the likely chords to be used in this key. The second half has been left to the student to complete. Apply this procedure to all pieces to be played, and try to be aware of the chords you are playing during the performance of the piece. Particularly before **sightreading** any piece, try to sum up the chords and the harmonies in each bar. Keep in mind that chord notes are usually found on the strong beats of the bar.

Refer to: • Contemporary Chord Workbook p 4

HOW TO SPOT THE CHORDS

A) If the chord is in block form go straight to Stage 4.

B) If the chord appears in broken form (split up between the hands) the procedure for finding the chord is as follows:

Stage 1. Arrange all the notes of the section in either skips or skip-plus-ones, leaving out the scale notes which pass between the chord notes on the weak beats.

Stage 2. If there are any notes doubled up between the hands, delete them so that you are left with only one of each note name.

Stage 3. Bring the three remaining notes into close proximity (position) so that they can be played with one hand.

Stage 4. Invert the chord till you come to the ROOT Position.

Stage 5. The chord name (the lowest note in Root Position) should now match one of the chord names in the table. If it does so, it is the correct chord.

Stage 6. Write the chord name in the box.

CHORD TABLE

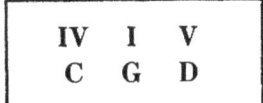

Figure 2   **DO NOT PLAY**

[sheet music]

Practice this new skill: Analyse the chords used in the arrangement of *I Saw Three Ships* on p17 of *Dexter's Easy Piano Pieces*.

*From this lesson onwards always complete the **Table of Primary Chords** for each piece, or if the numerals are not given, do the complete Chord Table for yourself. Where the instruction is on the page, find the chords of the table in the piece and write the chord names above each bar, as shown on page 41.*

The Key Signature (Key Sign)

The number of sharps or flats at the beginning of the stave along with the lowest final note in the bass part indicate the key or scale the music is written in.

Play the scale and chord of the key before playing each piece. This will enable you to find the keyboard pattern for the key and allow you to place the fingers along the pattern before commencing to play. When playing pieces that use sharps or flats, shift the hands further in over the black notes so that the fingers sit comfortably on the keys. Note whether the fingers should fall over the upper or lower section of the scale pattern and place them accordingly.

For further practice in this key, transpose the pieces on pages 21 and 22 to the key of D.

13. THREE FOR THE ROAD

WRITE CHORD TABLE HERE

KEY D

Practise these interval exercises on the scale pathways that you know, as well as on the white keys.

SIXTHS

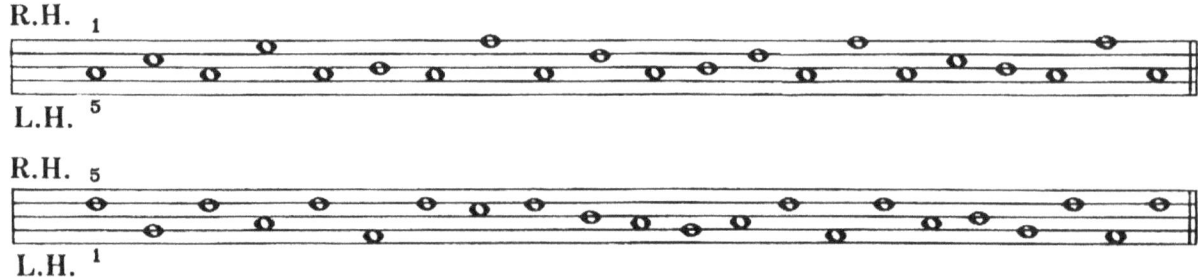

The ANACRUSIS. (Also known as Upbeat or Pickup).

This is an incomplete bar at the beginning of the piece, usually the last few beats of the bar. The remaining beats of the bar are found as the first few beats of the last bar. Thus together they make up a full bar. Ana means before, therefore an Anacrusis is the unaccented pick-up note or notes that precede the next Down beat. (Beat 1 of the next bar). The action a conductor makes on this beat is an Upward motion; hence the term Upbeat.

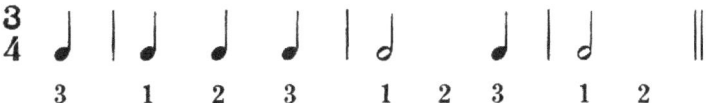

Transpose Finger Play (No. 3) on page 23 to the key of D Major. For No. 14 and No.3 both hands will be playing on the lower section of the scale pattern. No. 14 also includes an extension to the sixth.

14. STRUTTIN' ON SIXTH STREET

COMPLETE THE CHORD TABLE

IV	I	V

Expand your repertoire in the key of D Major:
* Dexter's Easy Piano Pieces p19, 20&22

INTERVALS. 7ths and OCTAVES. (8ves)

Interval Families

Space to Space   or   Line to Line

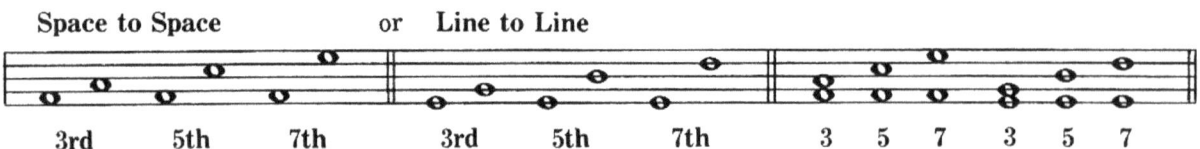

Space to Line   or   Line to Space

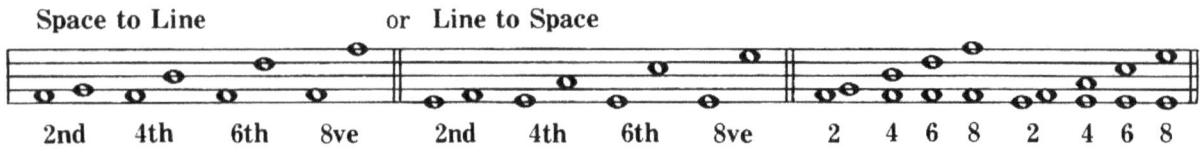

- Note that the seventh is always written line to line or space to space.
  It looks similar to the skip and the jump. Stretch one step further than the sixth.

When moving from a 'jump' (5th) to a '7th', skim the finger lightly over the cracks between the keys to help judge the distance.

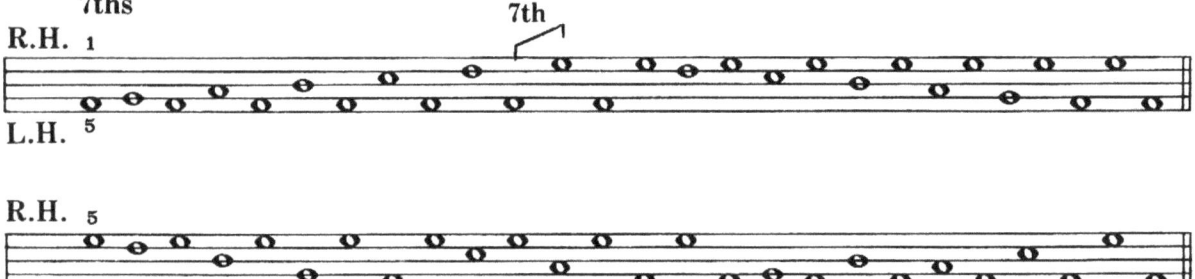

- The Octave is as far as most people can comfortably span. It is one step further than the seventh.

Note that it is always written from line to space or vice-versa similar to the sixth, skip-plus-one (fourth) and step.

The letter names of notes an octave apart are the same.

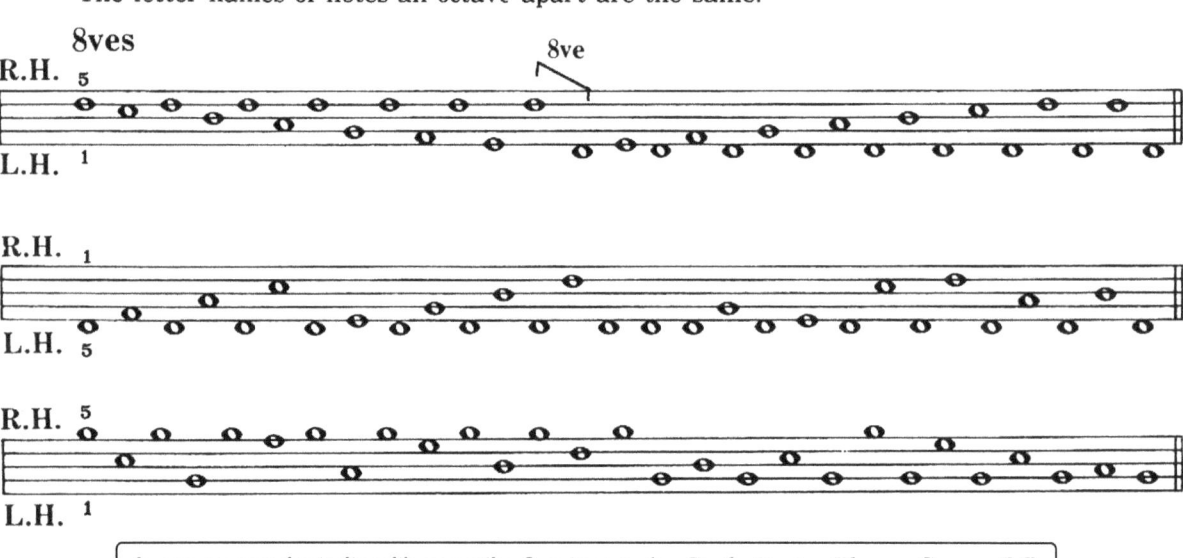

> Improve your dexterity with sevenths & octaves: play *Daily Dexter-Flexers Groups 5-7*

LISTEN HERE!

Play the following intervals:

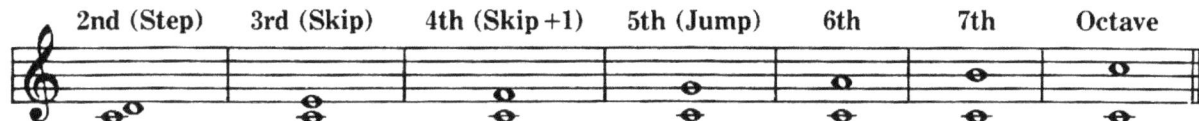

Write in which ones sound:
- (a) Pleasant but open and bare. ....
- (b) Pleasant and sweet. ....
- (c) Harsh and clashy. ....

Listen to the difference in sound between the intervals (distances) of a '6th', '7th' and '8ve'. Use your 'Ear' to tell you if you have landed on the right note or not. Do not look at your hands. Only then will the hands learn to judge the interval with confidence and as a most important side benefit you will have helped to train the ear to discriminate more carefully.

Refer to: • Contemporary Aural Course - Preparatory For Beginners, Set One & Set Two

Interval Exercises.

These exercises involve two hand positions. Keep your hand position until a fingering is indicated, then place the required finger on the note and retain the new hand position. I have written them without a clef to discourage reading the note names. Play them in different areas of the keyboard. When playing pieces from other books, use this approach when reading any piece of music, even to the extent of editing the printed fingering yourself. Use a correction fluid to block out any unnecessary fingering so that when a fingering appears it **must** be observed because it **involves a change in hand position**. In the long run this procedure will simplify the process of reading for you.

CHANGING HAND POSITIONS

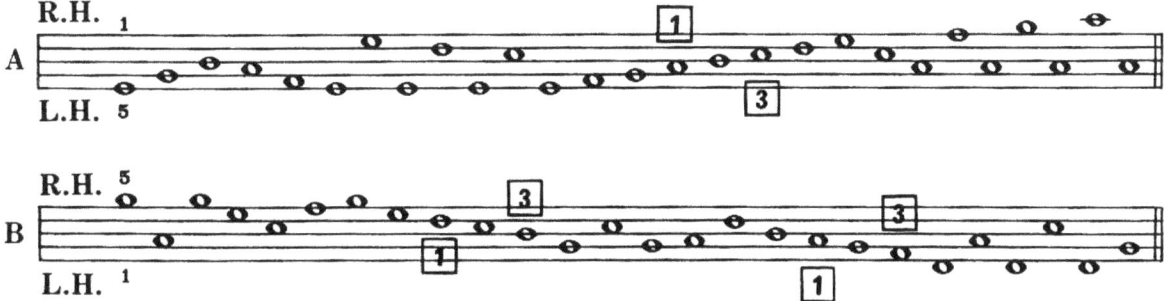

Refer to: • Daily Dexter-Flexers pp 21-27

OCTAVE HOPPING

Pick any starting note and move up and down the keyboard by intervals of an octave. Practise changing fingers while holding the note down. Swap either the thumb over to where the 5th finger was or vice-versa, and feel the next octave.

Test yourself by doing it with your eyes closed and letting your ears tell you if you are playing the right note or not.

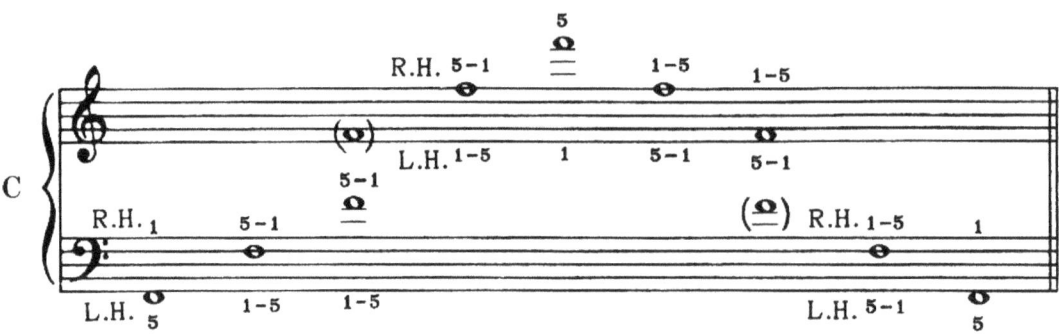

Refer to: • Dexter's Easy Piano Pieces p 30

INTERVAL READING USING ACCIDENTALS

Intervals usually derive from the scale in which the piece is written. When reading intervals it should be no problem to sharpen or flatten an interval when accidentals are indicated by adjusting the appropriate finger up or down by a semitone. Read the interval first then adjust the individual finger for the accidental. Make sure that the other fingers stay in position.

Talk the intervals with accidentals through in this manner: "Step with a Flat", or "Skip with a Sharp" and so on.

START ON C OR G ONLY

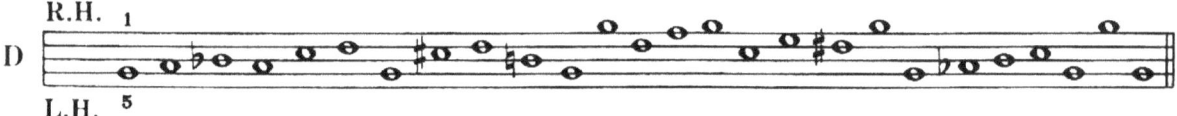

Refer to: • Dexter's Easy Piano Pieces p 32 - No. 32, p 36 and p 37

RIVER SONG

Before playing this piece, play the Major Scale of the Key in both Similar and Contrary Motion forms.

Take a good look at the pattern of **Black** notes for each hand. Make sure that you adjust the fingers onto the correct **Black** notes when the **thumb** goes **under** and puts the hand in a new position or when the third **finger** goes **over** and puts the hand in a new position.

Try playing this piece in the scales of C,G,D and E as well. Find your starting note and from there read the steps. Adjust the Black notes to suit each particular scale. (This process is known as Transposition or Transposing.)

Refer to the *Guide Notes* on page 65

15. RIVER SONG

COMPLETE THE CHORD TABLE

IV	I	V

Pictorial Pattern for A Major Contrary Motion Scale

Refer to: • Pictorial Patterns for Keyboard Scales and Chords pp 12-15

STACCATO

The style of playing used in this book this far has been the Legato style of playing where each note is smoothly connected to the next. In contrast to Legato playing there is another style of playing known as STACCATO playing. When playing in a Staccato manner, each note is detached from the next and played in a crisp manner, with the fingers bouncing off the keys.

STACCATO DOTS. When notes are to be played in a Staccato fashion small Staccato dots are placed either above or below the note depending on where the note head is written. (Do not confuse them with the dots placed behind notes, which indicate that the note is to be held for half as long again.) As well, a whole section may be marked with the word STACCATO in which case every note will be played in this fashion.

There are THREE ways to play Staccato Notes.
(1) With the **fingers** only.
(2) Bouncing the **hand** from the wrist.
(3) Bouncing the **forearm** from the elbow.

The **First** style is used for single note passages. Each finger lightly touches a key and then bounces off.

FINGER STACCATO

The **Second** style is used when two notes are played at the same time. The wrist is used in the same manner as when bouncing a ball.

WRIST STACCATO   EITHER HAND

The **Third** style is used when a full chord has to be played Staccato. Keep the fingers set in the position above the keys and bounce the forearm from the elbow, always keeping the line from the knuckles to the elbow straight.

FOREARM STACCATO

Staccato

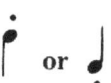

 Expand your repertoire in the key of A Major:
play *Dexter's Easy Piano Pieces* p22

16. CRISP AND CRUNCHY

Leave crotchet rest boxes blank.

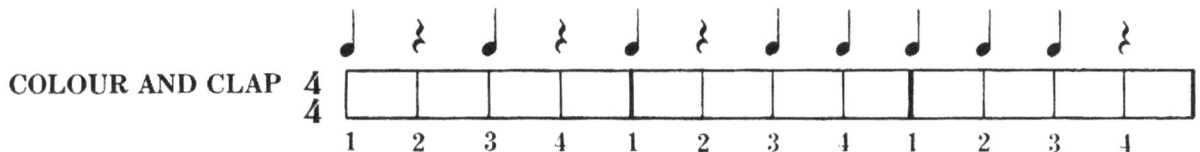

COLOUR AND CLAP

WRITE CHORD TABLE HERE

Practice Procedure
First play this with a legato touch to establish the intervals and keyboard pattern. When secure, add the staccato touch.

KEY A USE FINGER STACCATO

 **Improve your dexterity:** play *Daily Dexter-Flexers* p28-31

B and F MAJOR SCALES

This lesson B major and F major Scales can be added to those previously covered. Both these scales are similar in fingering to the first five (C, G, D, A, E) but contain **changes** in fingering to **one hand**.

B major

In B major due to the large number of black notes — 5 sharps: F C G D A — the left hand is forced to use a different fingering to avoid placing a thumb on one of those black notes. The only white notes are B and E. The logical place to put the thumb is on these notes. Thus the fingering becomes L.H. 4 3 2 1 4 3 2 1 ascending; that is — two groups of four fingers instead of the previous fingering which was a group of five and a group of three — 5 4 3 2 1 3 2 1. The right hand retains the same fingering as C major (3 + 5).

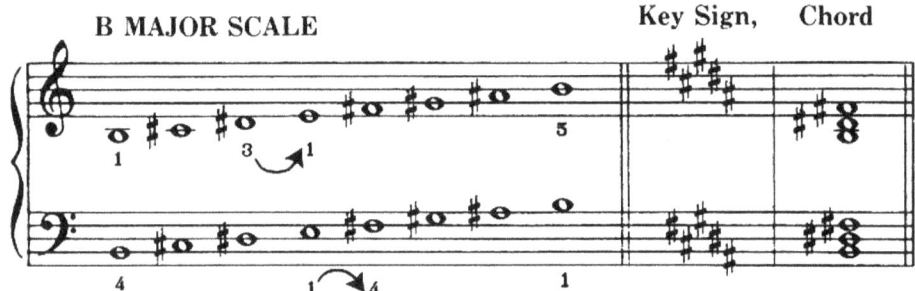

F Major

F major is the first scale with a flat that I have presented. That flat is B flat and because it is the fourth note in the scale, the **right** hand is forced to use two groups of four, that is 1 2 3 4 1 2 3 4. Again the reverse applies and the **left** hand uses C major fingering (5 + 3).

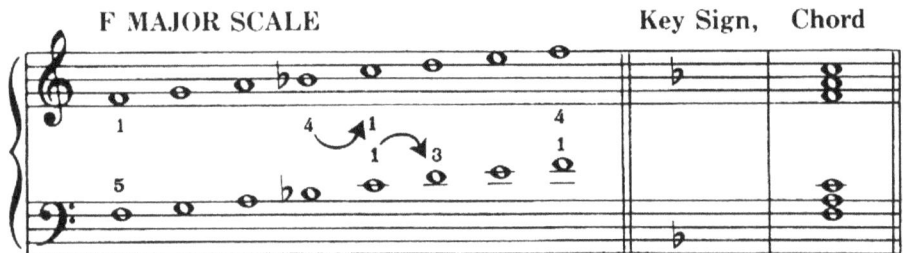

Remember, when playing scales avoid placing thumbs on black notes.
All scales should be played ascending and descending.

See page 67 for the Keyboard Patterns for these scales

BROKEN CHORDS

Here is F Major chord in both Block and Broken forms. It is very easy to learn chords in Broken form by simply splitting the Block chords so that the bottom, middle and top notes of each chord are played one at a time.

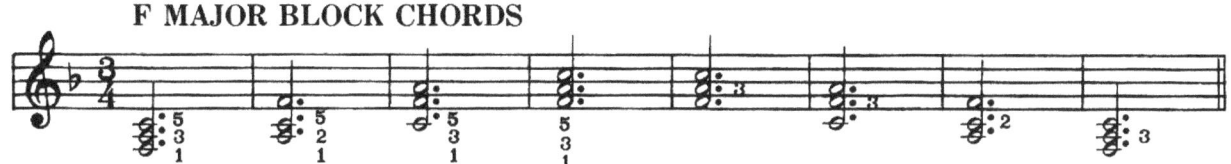

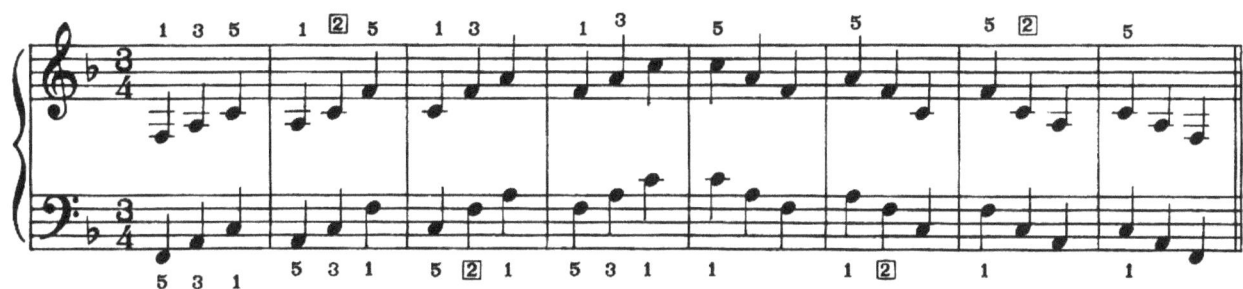

MUSIC SPEED READING AND TRANSPOSITION

To become a music speed reader, practice these interval exercises on the scale pathways that you know, as well as on the white keys.

SEVENTHS

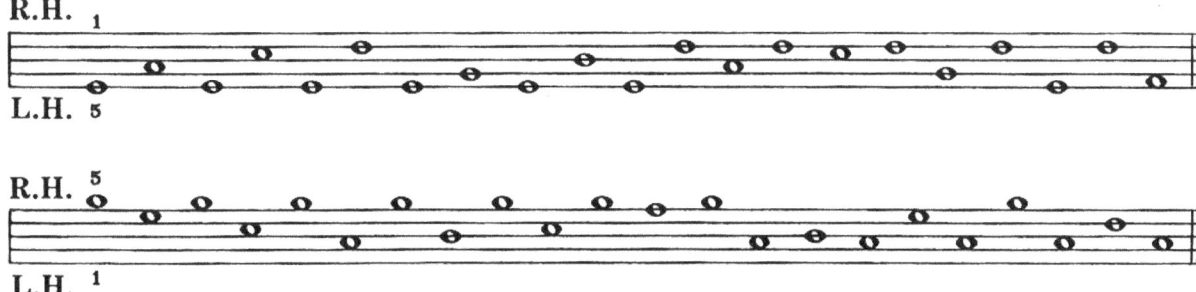

TWELVE-BAR BLUES

Here is an example of a basic Twelve-Bar Blues pattern. It uses the Primary Chords of the key in a particular order. Can you see how many bars of each chord are used? At this stage, use one chord per bar in the right hand. If the chord continues for more than one bar, change inversions for the following bars. You can choose to go up or down. If the chord name changes, connect the chord to the nearest inversion of the following chord. If there is a note in common, keep it in the same position (Bottom, Middle or Top) in both chords. In the long run this is the easiest way to get from one chord to another, as the hand does not have to alter its position. The chord change will sound smooth because the 'voice-leading' is correct.

The Blues is a fun way to get to know your Primary Chords in every key. Try transposing the chord sequence of this blues to a few different keys.

For detailed information on the Twelve Bar Blues Form refer to *'The Blues and Boogie-Woogie'*.

TWELVE-BAR BLUES IN C

COMPLETE THE CHORD TABLE

◇ - short hand for a BLOCK CHORD lasting four beats

> **Expand your repertoire of Blues pieces:**
> *Dexter's Easy Piano Pieces* p32
> *Blues and Boogie-Woogie* p6-7, *Hot Trax* pp28-29

THE EASY WAY TO READ CHORDS

When reading chords, read by intervals across the bar, taking note of the movements between each chord. Notice whether the notes step up or down or stay the same. Think along the scale pathway for each key.

Special Note: In popular music, the convention is to write the chord symbol once only to cover one or more bars, until the harmony changes.

PRE-PRACTICE PROCEDURE

Play the scale of the key plus the primary chords of the key in all inversions.

17. 'A' WALTZ

Complete the table and write the chord names above each bar.

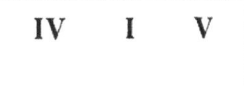

COLOUR AND CLAP

CHORD PROGRESSION PRACTICE
Play this chord progression in the keys of C, G, D and A with either hand or hands together.

Expand your chord skills: play *Dexter's Easy Piano Pieces* p23
It's Easy to Improvise – play the chord progressions on p5
& add left-hand chords to the tunes on p12 & 13.

B flat and E flat Major Scales and Chords.

You should now be ready to move on to the scales that begin on Black Notes. A basic rule to keep in mind when fingering these scales is that: 'after a black note the right hand thumb takes the first white note when ascending (↑) and the left hand does the same descending (↓)'.

Therefore B flat major having two flats — B flat and E flat — has the R.H. thumb on C and F, thus:

```
B♭       E♭        B♭
3  1  2  3  1  2  3  4
```

Note also the R.H. 4th finger on B flat.

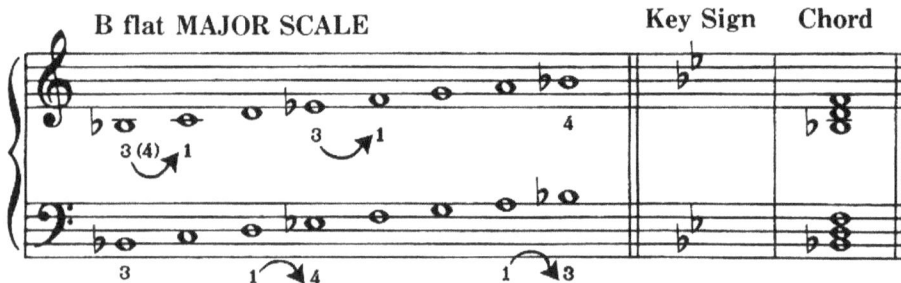

The left hand has the thumb on A and D, thus:

```
   B♭      E♭       B♭
*  3  2  1  4  3  2  1  3
```

* Learn this left hand fingering thoroughly as it is the same for B Flat, E Flat, A Flat and D Flat scales. If you compare the pictorial scale patterns on page 67 you will see that the third and seventh notes in each of these scales are white notes suitable for the Left Hand thumb to play.

KEY FACTS!

1) To find the keynote of the scale with one more flat, go *down* a jump or fifth from the upper tonic of the scale.

2) The Key Signature flats always follow this order: **B E A D G C F**
   Here is an easy rhyme to help you remember them in order:

                         Billy Edward And Daniel Go Cat Fishing

   Or the short version: **BEAD Goes Cat Fishing**

E flat major scale has three flats — B flat, E flat and A flat. Using the same principle as above, you will find that the right hand fingering is:

R.H. E♭   A♭ B♭   E♭
      3 1 2 3 4 1 2 3

Note again the Right Hand fourth finger on B flat. This will apply in all Black Notes Scales.

The left fingering is exactly the same as B flat.

3 2 1 4 3 2 1 3

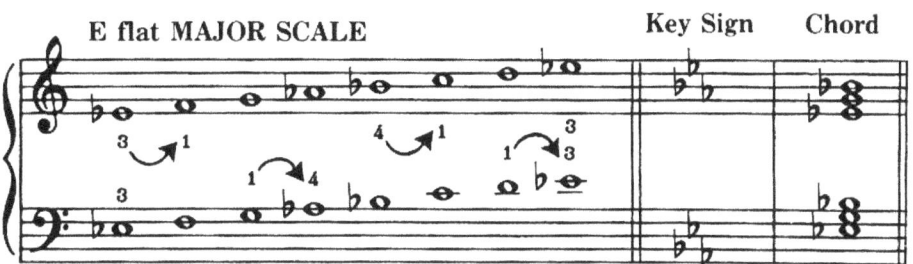

Do not forget to find the patterns of black
and white notes before playing a new scale.

Remember to play all scales ascending and descending.

Your practice routine should include the scales and chords listed below:

SIMILAR MOTION MAJOR SCALES -   F C G D A E B

CONTRARY MOTION MAJOR SCALES -   F C G D A E B

CHORDS AND INVERSIONS -   F C G D A E B

Refer to: • Pictorial Patterns for Keyboard Scales and Chords - for the fingering of these scales over two or more octaves.

Another type of repeat sign is the First and Second **time-bars.** Take the bars under the bracket marked 1 the first time and go straight to the bracket marked 2 the second time.

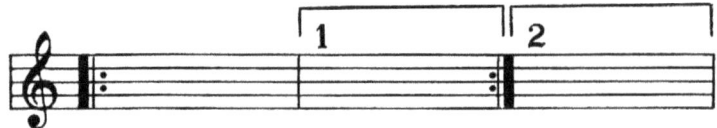

Also watch for **play 3 X's** and **time-bars** which look like this:

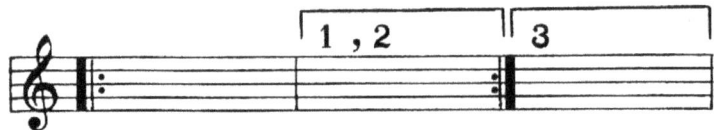

Something Extra
For keyboard practice in the chord movements for the Primary Chords beginning on the inversions of the Tonic Chord, refer to page 5 of *It's Easy To Improvise*. Play them in the written key and transposed to other keys.

18. SPACE INVADERS

Space Invaders, Space Invaders, Space Invaders — here they come,
Space Invaders, Space Invaders, come to knock out ev'ry one.

19. KUM BA YA

1. Kum ba ya, O Lord, Kum ba ya,
Kum ba ya, O Lord, Kum ba ya,
Kum ba ya, O Lord, Kum ba ya,
O Lord, Kum ba ya!

A flat and D flat Major Scales and Chords.

On page 54 the scales of B flat and E flat were introduced. Following the same method of working out the fingering, one finds that A flat major and D flat major have the **same left hand fingering** as B flat major: 3 2 1 4 3 2 1 3 ascending. The **right hand** fingering for A flat major which has 4 flats (B E A D) is:

A flat	B flat		D flat	E flat			A flat
3	4	1	2	3	1	2	3

Note again the 4th finger on B flat.

Do not forget to find the patterns of black and white notes before playing a new scale. See Figure 1 for D Flat and A Flat scales and chords.

In D Flat major which has five flats, B Flat, E Flat, A Flat, D Flat and G Flat, the right hand fingering will be 2 3 1 2 3 4 1 2 ascending. At this stage it is easier to remember the white notes than the black ones. D Flat major has only 2 white notes F and C, and in both hands the thumbs play these notes. As a result this scale is easier to co-ordinate than a scale with only three black notes such as A major. The old myth of black note scales being hard, came from those students who had not been taught these scales until the third or fourth year of study, by which time a massive MENTAL BLOCK had formed against scales with more than 3 sharps or flats.

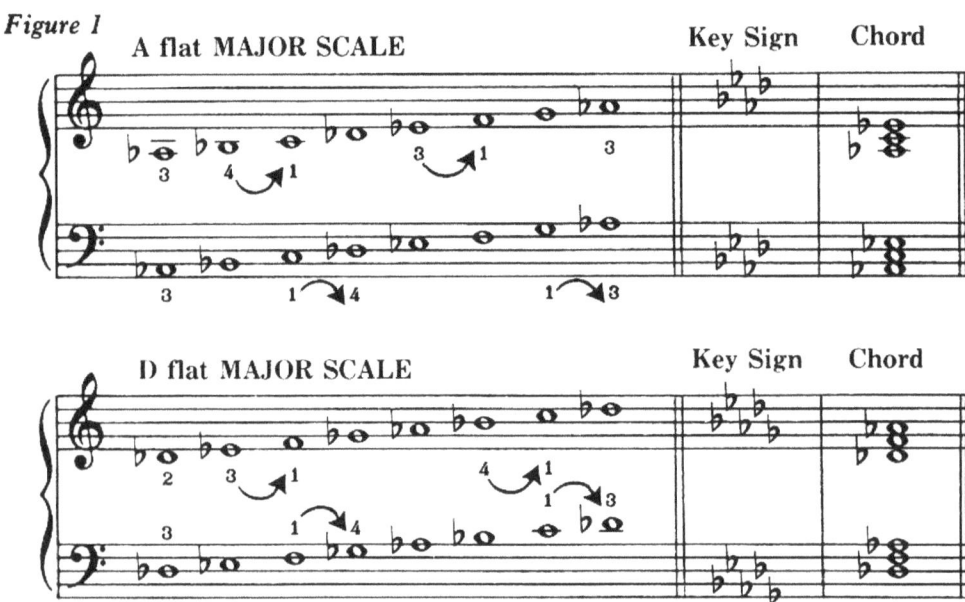

Figure 1

Play separately then together.   Remember the white notes.

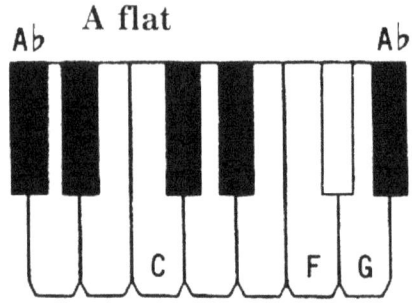
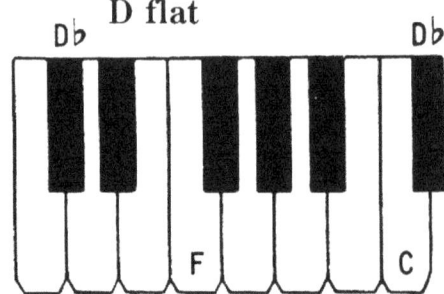

INSTANT TRANSPOSITION

- **Find your starting note and from there read the
  interval along the keyboard pattern for the scale.**

Transpose 'Love Somebody' to the keys of G, D, A and E using the lower section of each scale pattern. To find the chords for the new key, write a chord table to discover chord I and V.

20. LOVE SOMEBODY (YES I DO)

Play one chord per bar in the Left Hand beginning on C chord in the First Inversion.

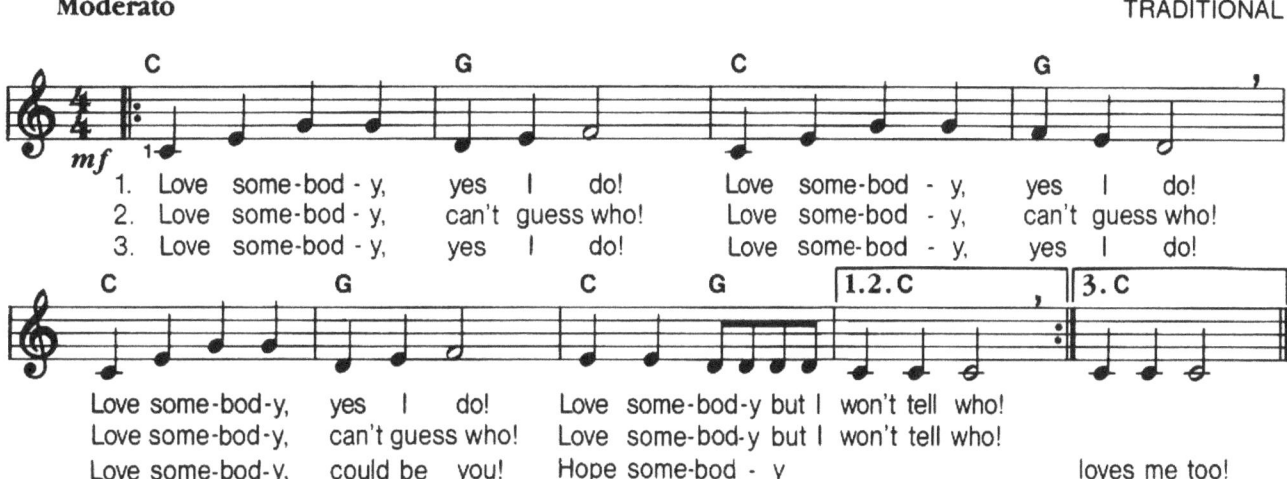

MUSIC SPEED READING AND TRANSPOSITION

Here are some lines of music using the wider intervals, and the less usual time signature of $\frac{5}{4}$

Play them in several different areas of the keyboard in several white note patterns (this will give either a major or a modal sound). Continue reading by intervals. Next, transpose them to the keys of G, D, A and E.

> **Expand your rhythm skills:**
> *Contemporary Theory Primer* p24&26 for practical rhythm exercises in Odd Times
> *Kerin Bailey's *Rhythm Unravelled*: clap rhythm patterns to CD backing tracks

SEVENTHS

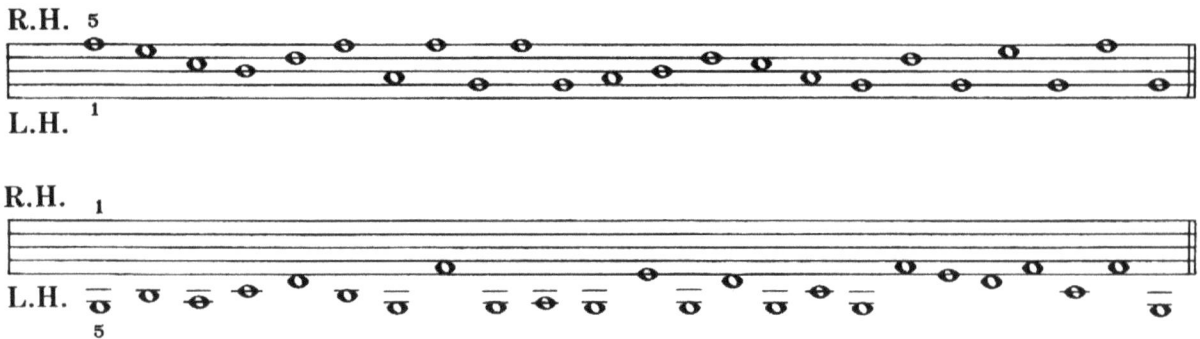

Preparatory Exercise: In order to establish the keyboard pattern for this piece, play the first line of intervals (using octaves) on page 44, transposed to the key of E. Teachers are advised to use an 'Interval Drill' with their students, calling out the required interval taken from either end of the scale pattern.

EIGHTH NOTES OR QUAVERS (♪ or ♫)

Two quavers equal one crotchet. In $\frac{2}{4}$ count: 1 + 2 +. In $\frac{3}{4}$ count: 1 + 2 + 3 +.

In $\frac{4}{4}$ count: 1 + 2 + 3 + 4 +. The '+' sign is short for the word 'AND'.

21. SEVENTH HEAVEN

♪ = USE RED and PINK ALTERNATING   Colour: 1st quaver — red
                                                                                                      2nd quaver — pink   etc.

WRITE CHORD TABLE HERE   COLOUR AND CLAP

KEY E

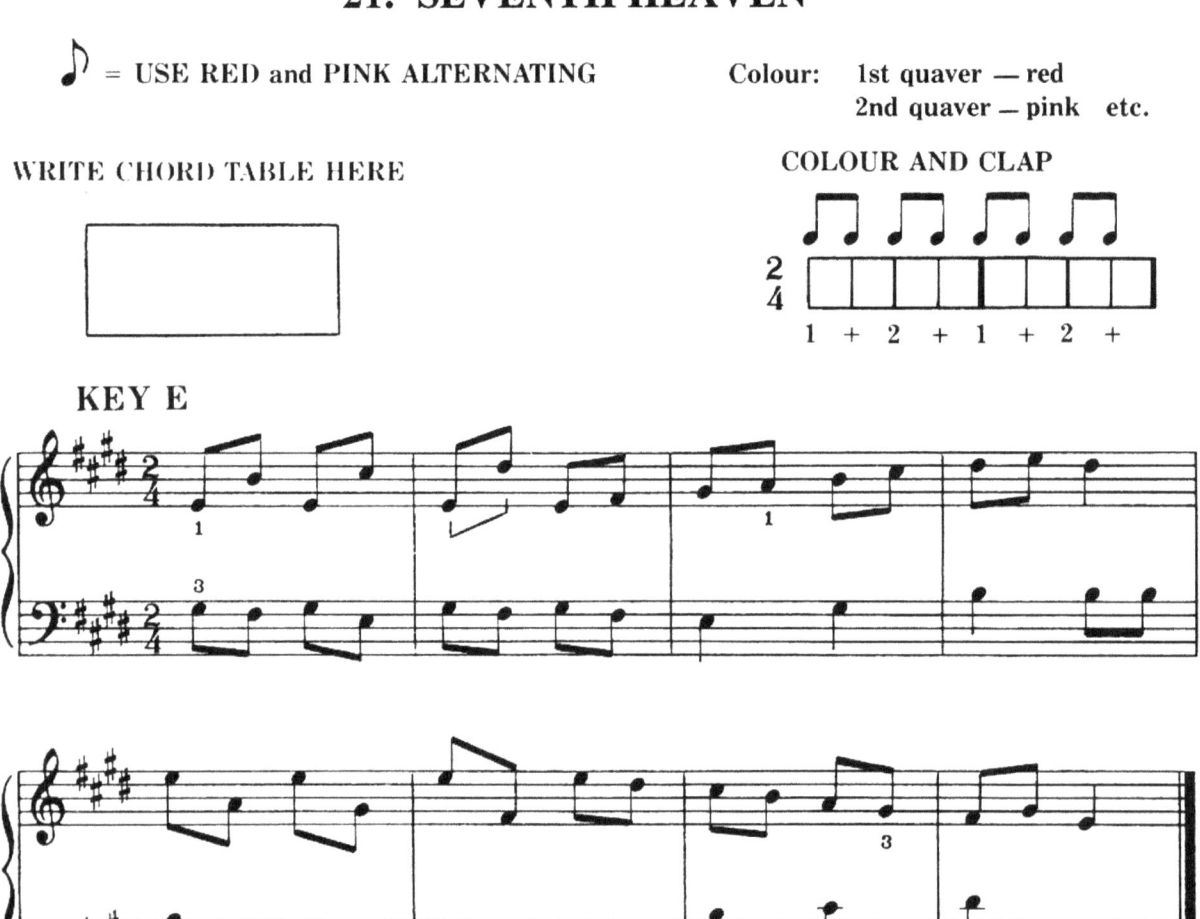

Practise these interval exercises on the scale pathways that you know, as well as on the white keys.

OCTAVES

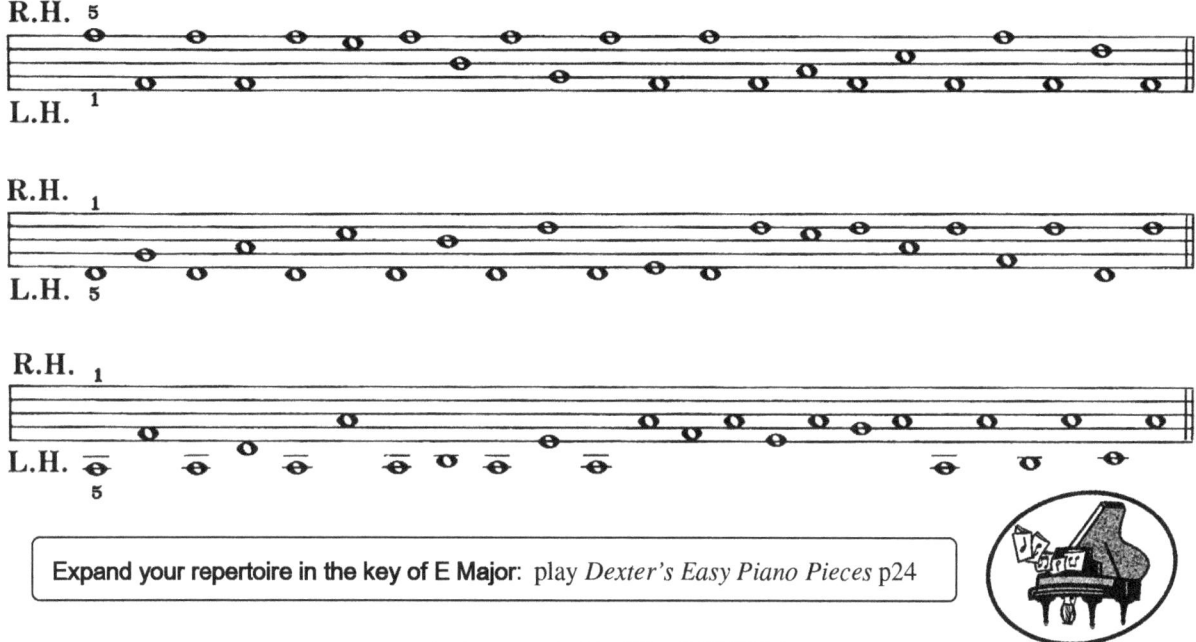

Expand your repertoire in the key of E Major: play *Dexter's Easy Piano Pieces* p24

22. OCTAVIUS' OPUS

COMPLETE THE CHORD TABLE

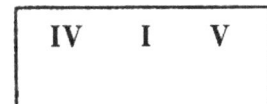

COLOUR AND CLAP

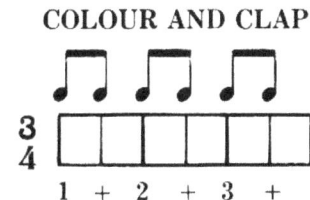

F Sharp Major Scale and Chord

The last scale in the circle to be covered is F sharp major. It has a key signature of 6 sharps — F, C, G, D, A, E. I have left this scale to a section on its own as the left hand fingering differs from the other scales starting on black notes (B flat, E flat A flat, D flat). When you map out the black notes of F sharp scale you find that the only white notes available for the thumb are B and E sharp (same as F). Thus the only possible fingering for the right hand is 2 3 4 1 2 3 1 2 and for the left hand is 4 3 2 1 3 2 1 4. Note again that the right hand has the 4th finger on A sharp (same as B flat). This scale also produces the only Major Chord with all black notes. See Figure 1 for F sharp major scale and chord.

Figure 1

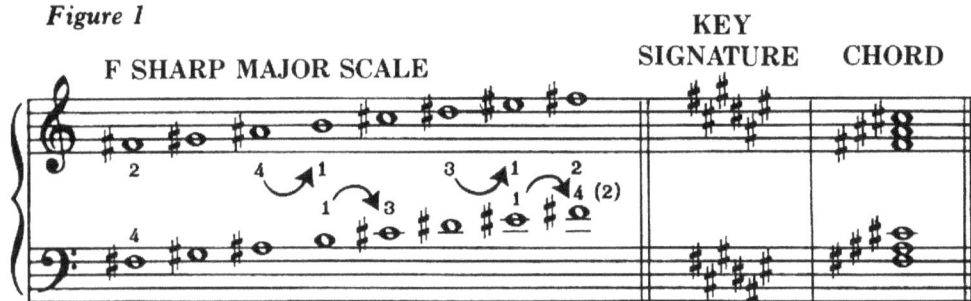

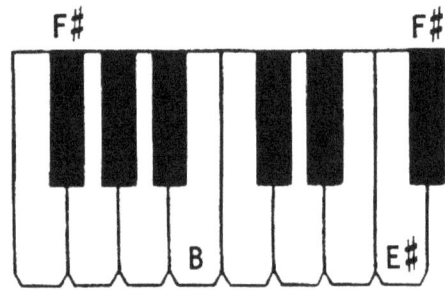

Once all the major scales have been learnt, practice them in the routine given on page 66.

**Special Note on the fingering for scales which
use all five black notes (B, F sharp & D flat)**

- Both hands will use fingers 3 2 or 2 3 for the group of two black notes - Peace Sign.
- Both hands will use fingers 4 3 2 or 2 3 4 for the group of three black notes - Boy-scout Salute.
- Both hands will use finger 1 for all the white notes.

Play each scale in 'chunks' noting the 'gestalt' (whole view) patterns that occur. This makes the learning of the above scales a very easy matter.

CYCLE OF FIFTHS

The benefit of learning all twelve scales in a short space of time, is that one is able to see how the scales relate to one another and fit into the Circle (or Cycle) of Fifths, and that each scale is as easy as the next.

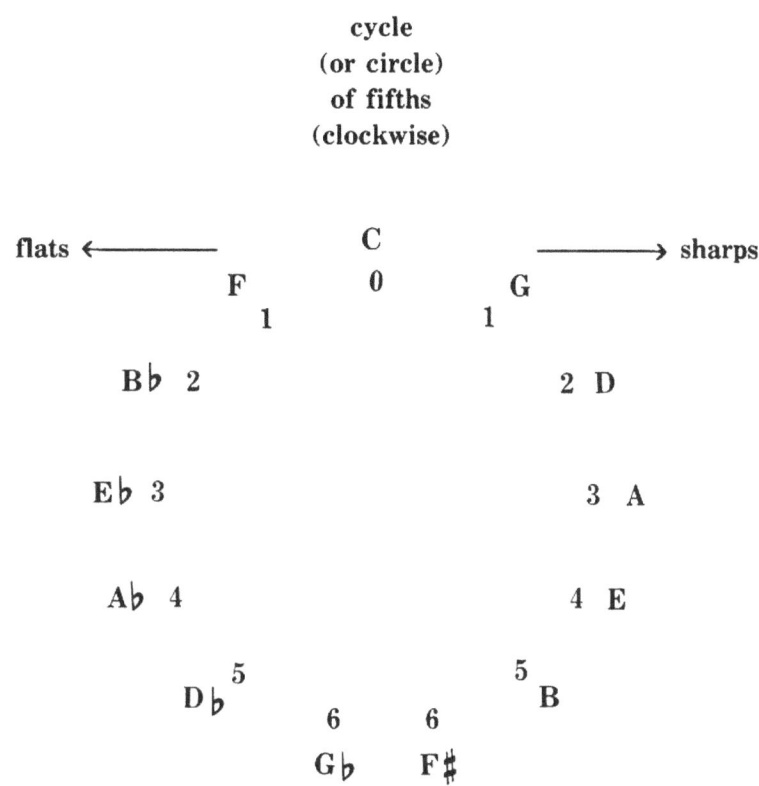

Try to think of scales as **pathways** on the piano, each one having its own shape. Some have only a few black notes in certain patterns and others have only two or three **white** notes emerging through the black notes.

When you are playing a piece in **A major** for instance, there will be a key signature at the beginning of the line, but you will not have the sharps written in front of each specific note.

All the steps move up and down the **pathway** or **pattern** of A major scale. So you must know the **pathway** before trying to play the piece in that key.

When learning the order of scales and sharps and flats as presented in the Cycle of Fifths, it is useful to memorise these seven letters: F,C,G,D,A,E,B. All the scales in the cycle appear in this order, either with sharps or flats after each letter name or with the letter name only. If the Cycle were written out in a straight line using all possible Key names, that is, using alternative names for the scales you already know, it would look like this:

F♭, C♭, G♭, D♭, A♭, E♭, B♭, F, C, G, D, A, E, B, F♯, C♯, G♯, D♯, A♯, E♯, B♯.

Also, the order of Sharps follows this sequence exactly and the order of Flats is the same sequence read backwards.

THE CHROMATIC SCALE

There is one other important scale to learn at this stage. This is the **Chromatic** scale. The name comes from the Greek word Chroma meaning colour. The scale uses all the black and white notes in succession. All the black notes are played with the 3rd finger in either hand and most of the white notes are played with the thumb. The exception is when there are two white notes together ie:— E F and B C. Here the 1st and 2nd fingers are used so that the next black note can again be played with the 3rd finger. If you start on C the fingering is as follows:

Right hand (ascending)

1 3 1 3 1̂ 2 3 1 3 1 3 1̂ 2
        E F   B C

Left Hand (ascending)

1 3 1 3 2 1 3 1 3 1 3 2 1
        E F   B C

Chromatic Scale

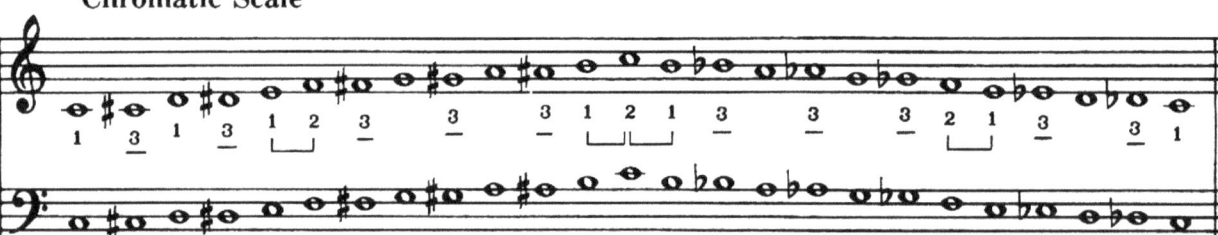

GUIDE NOTES FOR THE TEACHER

pp 14-31

Transposition: As all the material on these pages is written within the five-finger hand position, it is suitable for transposition to (a) other white-note positions (giving modal sounds) and (b) to the first five notes of any major or minor scale.

Two simple transpositions that can be used for the beginning student are to:
    1) transpose any C positions which use the first five notes of C Scale (Ionian Mode) to G position (that is: the first five notes of G Scale).
    2) transpose any F Lydian positions (i.e. last five notes of C scale) to C position (Tunes 4, 5 and 8).

pp 21-31

Cuing: For beginning students, it may be useful to pencil in the final notes of the first system* in front of the first notes of the second system. By bringing the notes closer together, students will find it easier to continue reading from one system to the other. Once the student is more experienced this will no longer by required (*system = a collection of staves e.g. a great staff).

p 23

Playing detached repeated notes in one hand and varying intervals smoothly in the other: This skill is required for *No. 3 (Finger Play)*. Before playing this piece, rehearse this skill in Daily Dexter Flexers (p 13). Use the eighth note counting 1 + 2 + 3 + 4 + so that the finger can be lifted off on the 'and' before a *repeated note or same*.

p 31

Direction Concepts: The two pieces on this page should be viewed with a focus on the combined direction between the hands. It is useful to say the directions while playing: In, Out, Up, Down, Same or Oblique. The interval reading concepts here are very useful, as the hands are set wide apart and it would be very confusing to have to look at the fingers on the keyboard. Students are usually very comfortable playing with hands widely spaced when reading intervallically and concentrating on direction. Ask the student to trace the directions by touching the music on the page with the thumb and forefinger of one hand, as demonstrated on the *Contemporary Piano Method DVD*.

p 37

Extra practice in new keys: As the new keys are introduced, suggest to the student to play the early pieces (*No's 1, 2 and 3*) in the new key. Encourage students to place their fingers over the keyboard pattern for the scale and then point out that the reading by intervals is exactly the same. Refer also to *Daily Dexter-Flexers* groups 1-3, and *Dexter's Easy Piano Pieces* pages 7-13, which can easily be transposed.

If required, the student should draw his/her own pictorial scale pattern on the page near the music. This can be done each time a piece is presented in a new key until such time as the keyboard pattern is fully understood.

pp 42-43

Adding the interval of a sixth: By now the change-over student (that is - one who has read by note-names previously and has changed to reading by intervals) should be comfortable with the new system and be able to play in the written key (home key) using the intervals and pattern for the key as the primary means of reading. If they are not reading by intervals by now they will miss the interval of a **sixth**.

p 47

Hand Position thinking: The focus of this page is to feel the two hand positions of the scale. Either the lower segment of the scale pattern or the upper segment. The main challenge is to attain the new position. Once in position the reading is straightforward.

Visualisation: In order to establish a solid concept of the keyboard pathway for a scale, or for a section of music, block out the scale segment, holding all the notes down. Then close eyes and visualise the hand on the keyboard using the information relayed by touch. Once you begin to read the music be aware of the tactile picture being relayed by the hands, so there is no need to look down at the hands while playing.

Incorporating the gestalt view of music: From this point on in the method, use hand positioning as a means to learn all pieces. Practice position changes, five-finger shapes and chord shapes, in chunks before playing the notes as written. Expand and consolidate all areas presented in the method by integrating pieces from the support materials referred to throughout the book.

SUMMARY of SCALE FINGERING

		Left Hand	Right Hand
Group 1.	C G D A E.	5 4 3 2 1 3 2 1	1 2 3 1 2 3 4 5
Group 2.	B	4 3 2 1 4 3 2 1	Same as Group 1
	F	Same as Group 1	1 2 3 <u>4</u> 1 2 3 4
Group 3.	B flat	3 2 1 4 3 2 1 3	<u>4</u> 1 2 3 1 2 3 <u>4</u>
	E flat	" " " " " " " "	3 1 2 3 <u>4</u> 1 2 3
	A flat	" " " " " " " "	3 <u>4</u> 1 2 3 1 2 3
	D flat	" " " " " " " "	2 3 1 2 3 <u>4</u> 1 2
Group 4.	F sharp	4 3 2 1 3 2 1 3	2 3 <u>4</u> 1 2 3 1 2

N.B.
Right Hand **Fourth** Finger on B flat (A sharp) in all scales in which the <u>4</u> is printed in heavy type.

TRIAD FINGERING

	Root Pos.	1st Inv.	2nd Inv.	Root Pos.
Right Hand	135	125	135	135
Left Hand	531	531	521	531

SUGGESTED PRACTICE ROUTINE

Once you have learnt all the Major Scales and Chords, practise them on a rotation system, taking **Five** different scales per day moving around the Cycle of Fifths. (See Page 63).

For instance:

	MONDAY	TUESDAY	WEDNESDAY	THURSDAY etc.
Similar Motion:	C,G,D,A,E.	B,F#,Db,Ab,Eb.	Bb,F,C,G,D.	A,E,B,F#,Db.
Contrary Motion:	B,F#,Db,Ab,Eb.	Bb,F,C,G,D.	A,E,B,F#,Db.	Ab,Eb,Bb,F,C.
Chords:	Bb,F,C,G,D.	A,E,B,F#,Db.	Ab,Eb,Bb,F,C.	G,D,A,E,B.
Chromatic Scale:	From C-C.	From Db-Db.	From D-D.	From Eb-Eb.

Within 3 days you have covered all 12 scales and by taking Five different scales per day you are seeing a slightly different group each day.

Refer to: • Pictorial Patterns for Keyboard Scales and Chords

MAJOR SCALE KEYBOARD PATTERNS

Read each column from **top** to bottom and notice how the patterns 'grow'. Observe how the position of the black note(s) remains the same, while an extra black note is added in each scale.

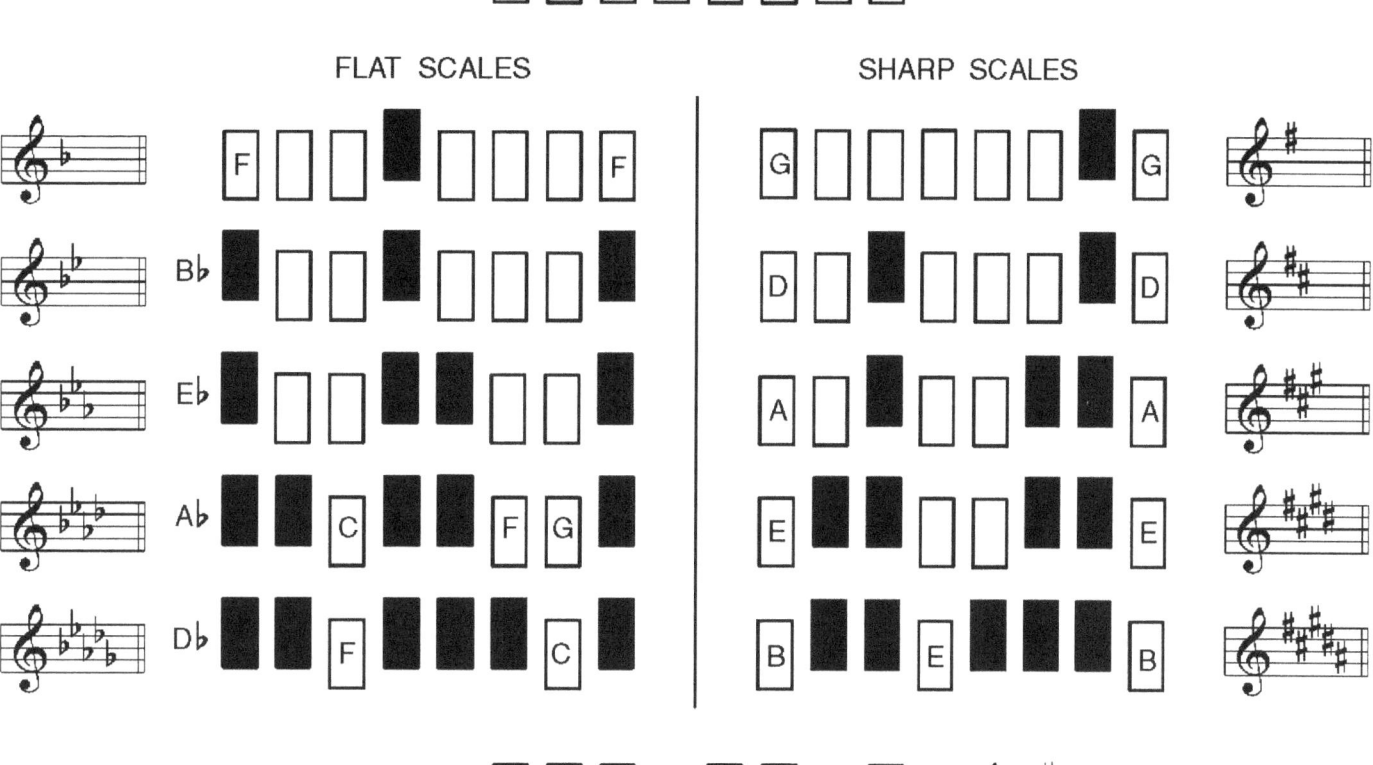

MAJOR CHORD SHAPES

Notice the mirror image shapes at opposite sides of the circle.

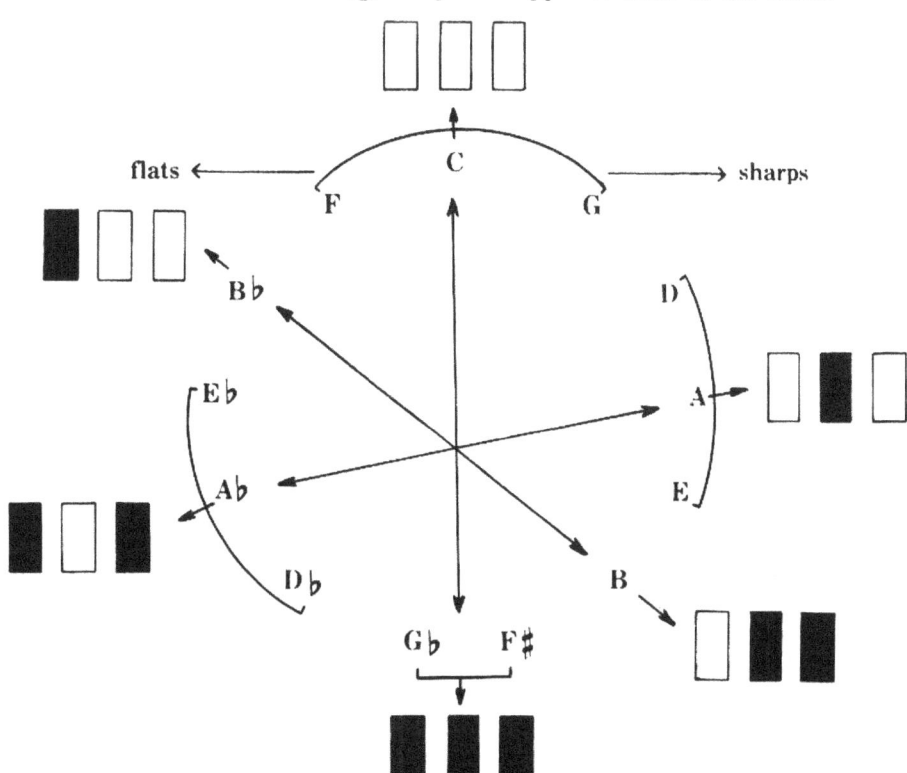

HANDY MANUSCRIPT PAGE

www.ingramcontent.com/pod-product-compliance
Lightning Source LLC
Chambersburg PA
CBHW081524160426
43195CB00015B/2480